A Taste of Challah

A Comprehensive Guide to Challah and Bread Baking   **Tamar Ansh**

ISBN-13: 978-1-58330-922-3
ISBN-10: 1-58330-922-5

Photography: Sharon Bentov
Graphic Design: Ben Gasner / Leah Green

Feldheim Publishers
POB 43163, Jerusalem, Israel
208 Airport Executive Park, Nanuet, NY 10954

www.feldheim.com

10 9 8 7 6 5 4 3 2 1

Printed in Israel

Published to encourage young women, older women, freshly Jewish, oldly Jewish, newly marrieds, oldly marrieds, and soon-to-be-marrieds everywhere.

Feel the excitement and fulfillment of your own special Shabbos challahs.

Participate in one of the three most important mitzvos given specifically to women.

Enjoyable, simple, and delicious!

Encourage others to do the same.

Just in case you are wondering...

YES.

All the recipes shown throughout this entire book really were home-made. We baked each and every item ourselves in order to prove to you, our readers, that each recipe really does work, and really does come out delicious.

Enjoy!

In Appreciation...

IN YOUR HANDS you now hold the work of many, many months and many wonderful people. Countless hours were spent testing recipes and developing techniques, of gathering and writing down tips and sound advice. On top of all that, before every photo session, there were literally weeks of baking and preparation, so that each item in this book would be displayed in its perfection. And we won't even mention all the eating that we had to do!

A book of this magnitude could not possibly have been done by one person alone. There were many special individuals along the way that brought this book to its completion.

My mother, Edith Shachter, has been making challahs (and all sorts of other things as well!) since my childhood. The wonderful smells in her kitchen prompted me to want to do the same in mine. The Yemenite breads and accompaniments – Kubana, Saluf, Chilba, Schug, Resek – were all done in conjunction with my friend, Malkie Sharabi. David Sasson of Sasson's Gourmet Cuisine, Manchester (formerly of Copenhagen), graciously donated the Sourdough Bread recipe, and he can be contacted at info@sassons.org. Mrs. Toby Gedult of Cleveland, Ohio, gave me the delectable Oatmeal Raisin Bread. Rochel Baumgarten is the young lady behind the Bread Basket pictures. The entire idea and the way it is woven, baked and displayed is her invention. The very first recipe in this book, "Always Perfect No Egg Challah," along with a few of the different shaping methods and several other recipes, first appeared in "Mishpacha Magazine." The beautiful silver Judaica items as well as the challah cover that is displayed in the photos on pages 184-185 were donated for photography purposes by Oter Yisroel (Tefilin & Judaica, Jerusalem, www.oter-israel.co.il)

Several of the dishes and baskets used in the photos were loaned to us by Shai Gift Shop, (5 Kanfei Nesharim St., Jerusalem, 02-652-1999).

Bassie Gruen gave me endless technical and editing advice during all the stages of this book's production. Her insightful comments tweaked many a paragraph.

And last, but most certainly not least, is my special, special friend in Beitar Illit who helped me tirelessly with baking, advice, testing of recipes, and her own expertise in areas of different flours and bread types, unstintingly giving me both her precious time and her knowledge.

A tremendous thank you goes to my proofreaders, Yocheved Krems and Deena Nataf. The beautiful and hard work of the graphic artist Leah Green shines throughout this book; it is due mainly to her, and to Ben Gasner of Ben Gasner Studio, Jerusalem, that this book is such an incredible masterpiece.

I am grateful to Mendy Feldheim and Eli Mayer Hollander of Feldheim Publishers for their enthusiastic support of this project from its initial stages over a year and a half ago.

The creative and outstanding work of my photographer, Sharon Bentov, is the touch that makes this book unique. Without him, this book would be absolutely lifeless. Each eye-catching photo is the product of his special talents.

A special thank you is reserved for my family, both the immediate members and those farther away. The excitement and encouragement they gave constantly kept me going all along. My husband, Reuven, deserves special note for handling many of the business aspects of this project, as well as for believing it would be a success before it was even off the ground.

Most of all I would like to thank Hashem Yisborach, G-d Above, for all the good He continuously showers upon me; for granting me so many wonderful opportunities, and seeing fit to imbue me with the various abilities and ideas needed to continue working in this field.

"אודך ה' אלוקי בכל לבבי, ואכבדה שמך לעולם"

Tamar Ansh
Tishrei 5767
Jerusalem

Contents

Introduction

[1] Picture-Perfect Challah Tips

[2] Seven Steps to Amazing Challah

[3] Large Challah Shapes

[4] Small Challah Shapes

[5] *Health Challah & Breads*

Stories

[6] *Specialty Breads*

[7] *Middle Eastern Breads & Accompaniments*

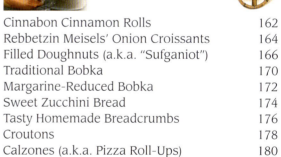

[8] *Fun & Different Ideas*

Halachos of Separating Challah

Measurements and Conversions

"And there was a continual blessing in her dough"

Bereishis / Genesis 24:67,
Commentary of Rashi

Separating Challah

For guidelines, see "Halachos of Separating Challah" at the end of this book.

These quantities are for white flour challah (for other kinds, see pages 190-191): For 2 lbs., 10 oz. to 3 lbs., 10 oz. (1.2–1.67 kilo) of flour, challah should be separated without a *brachah* • For 3 lbs., 10 oz. to 5 lbs. (1.67–2.25 kilo) of flour, challah should be separated. Some people recite a *brachah*, and some do not • For more than 5 lbs. (2.25 kilo) of flour, challah should be separated with a *brachah* • Separate a piece the size of a *kezayis*, i.e. half a standard egg.

Before separating challah, recite this blessing:

Taking challah is one of the three special mitzvos given exclusively to women. It is an eis ratzon (a very special time) before G-d in Heaven, and you should give yourself several minutes of private time when fulfilling the actual Biblical commandment of removing the dough (being "mafrish challah") to really pray for everything in your heart, and for all of the Jewish Nation in general.

Try to utilize this special opportunity to the best of your ability.

בָּרוּךְ אַתָּה יְיָ אֱלֹהֵינוּ מֶלֶךְ הָעוֹלָם אֲשֶׁר קִדְּשָׁנוּ בְּמִצְוֹתָיו וְצִוָּנוּ לְהַפְרִישׁ חַלָּה

some add: מִן הָעִסָּה

or alternatively: תְּרוּמָה

Blessed are You, Lord, our G-d, King of the Universe, Who has sanctified us with His commandments and commanded us to separate challah (from the dough).

BARUCH ATA ADONOY ELOHEINU MELECH HA-OLAM ASHER KEEDSHANU BE-MITZVOSAV VETZEEVANU LEHAFREESH CHALLAH (MIN HA-ISAH/TRUMAH).

Declare the separated piece to be challah by saying

הֲרֵי זוֹ חַלָּה or *"this is challah"*

Prayer for Separating Challah:

יְהִי רָצוֹן מִלְפָנֶיךָ יְיָ אֱלֹהֵינוּ וֵאלֹהֵי אֲבוֹתֵינוּ, שֶׁיִּבָּנֶה בֵּית הַמִּקְדָּשׁ בִּמְהֵרָה בְיָמֵינוּ, וְתֵן חֶלְקֵנוּ בְּתוֹרָתֶךָ, וְשָׁם נַעֲבָדְךָ בְּיִרְאָה כִּימֵי עוֹלָם וּכְשָׁנִים קַדְמוֹנִיּוֹת. וְעָרְבָה לַיְיָ מִנְחַת יְהוּדָה וִירוּשָׁלָיִם, כִּימֵי עוֹלָם וּכְשָׁנִים קַדְמוֹנִיּוֹת.

וִיהִי רָצוֹן מִלְפָנֶיךָ שֶׁהַמִּצְוָה שֶׁל הַפְרָשַׁת חַלָּה תִּתְחַשֵּׁב כְּאִלּוּ קִיַּמְתִּיהָ בְּכָל פְּרָטֶיהָ וְדִקְדּוּקֶיהָ, וְתֵחָשֵׁב הֲרָמַת הַחַלָּה שֶׁאֲנִי מְרִימָה כְּמוֹ הַקָּרְבָּן שֶׁהִקְרַב עַל הַמִּזְבֵּחַ שֶׁנִּתְקַבֵּל בְּרָצוֹן, וּכְמוֹ שֶׁלְּפָנִים הָיְתָה הַחַלָּה נְתוּנָה לַכֹּהֵן וְהָיְתָה זוֹ לְכַפָּרַת עֲווֹנוֹת, כָּךְ תִּהְיֶה לְכַפָּרָה לַעֲווֹנוֹתַי, וְאָז אֶהְיֶה כְּאִלּוּ נוֹלַדְתִּי מֵחָדָשׁ נְקִיָּה מֵחֵטְא וְעָווֹן – וְאוּכַל לְקַיֵּם מִצְוַת שַׁבָּת קֹדֶשׁ וְהַיָּמִים הַטּוֹבִים, עִם בַּעְלִי (וִילָדֵינוּ) לִהְיוֹת נִזּוֹנִים מִקְּדֻשַּׁת הַיָּמִים הָאֵלֶּה, וּמֵהַשְׁפָּעָתָהּ שֶׁל מִצְוַת חַלָּה יְהִיוּ יְלָדֵינוּ נִזּוֹנִים תָּמִיד מִיָּדָיו שֶׁל הַקָּדוֹשׁ בָּרוּךְ הוּא בְּרֹב רַחֲמָיו וַחֲסָדָיו, וּבְרֹב אַהֲבָה, וְשֶׁתִּתְקַבֵּל מִצְוַת חַלָּה כְּאִלּוּ נָתַתִּי מַעֲשֵׂר, וּכְשֵׁם שֶׁהִנְנִי מְקַיֶּמֶת מִצְוַת חַלָּה בְּכָל לֵב, כָּךְ יִתְעוֹרְרוּ רַחֲמָיו שֶׁל הַקָּדוֹשׁ בָּרוּךְ הוּא לְשָׁמְרֵנִי מִצַּעַר וּמִמַּכְאוֹבִים כָּל הַיָּמִים, אָמֵן:

MAY IT BE YOUR WILL, Eternal, our G-d, and the G-d of our forefathers, that the Temple be rebuilt speedily, in our days. Let our portion be together in Your Torah. And there we will serve You, with reverence and awe, as in days gone by, as in years long ago. And there we will sacrifice to Hashem, our G-d, the offerings of Yehudah and Yerushalayim, as in days gone by, as in years long ago.

MAY IT BE YOUR WILL, Eternal, our G-d, that the commandment of separating challah be considered as if I had performed it with all its details and ramifications. May my elevation of the challah be comparable to the sacrifice that was offered on the altar, which was acceptable and pleasing. Just as giving the challah to the Kohein in former times served to atone for sins, so may it atone for mine, and make me like a person reborn without sins. May it enable me to observe the holy Sabbath (or Festival of...) with my husband (and our children) and to become imbued with its holiness. May the spiritual influence of the mitzvah of challah enable our children to be constantly sustained by the hands of the Holy One, blessed is He, with His abundant mercy, loving-kindness, and love. Consider the mitzvah of challah as if I have given a tithe. And just as I am fulfilling this mitzvah with all my heart, so may Your compassion be aroused to keep me from sorrow and pain, always. Amen.

Dear Reader,

AS YOU LEAF through this book, you may be wondering – what prompted the idea for a book that centers on only challah and home bread baking?

Bread is an important staple in the diet of many people, and it can be used and served in a wide variety of ways. In fact, almost every culture has its own traditional breads. It is not for naught that bread is so often the main attraction at festive meals.

Even so, there is something singularly mystical and unique about the special Jewish bread called Challah.* The very word conjures up images of a warm kitchen, redolent with the aromas of long ago.

Baking challah is mentioned in Jewish liturgy countless times, and its importance and centrality to the Jewish home is often stressed. This special skill has been passed down over the course of many years, from mother to daughter, generation after generation.

The tradition of baking challah has survived upheavals and migrations, and continues to entrance us to this very day.

And, although each sector of Jewish culture has its own claims to their particular customs relating to challah, the sanctity attached to this special form of bread surpasses that of any other. And that is why this book was written.

In *A Taste of Challah*, the art of challah-making, and a broad selection of bread recipes, have been brought together to add pleasure and skill to your baking experience. It is my aim to take this art and de-mystify it, so that everyone, everywhere, can enjoy baking challah and bread. It will no longer be relegated to the bakery or the neighbor down the block who has over twenty years' experience. It will now belong to you, too, in your very own kitchen, in your very own home.

* The word "challah" is a Hebrew word that refers to the portion of dough set aside for the Kohein (Priest) during the time of the Temple. With time, the word has come to mean the festive Jewish Sabbath bread itself.

IMPORTANT NOTE:

*A **Taste of Challah** is not just a cookbook. It is a comprehensive guide to challah and bread baking. As such, a careful reading of the beginning chapters on how to make the dough workable and perfect — the absolute prerequisite to any good bread — is essential.*

After you have perused those aspects thoroughly, you can then continue learning the art of challah by trying out the many different ways and customs of shaping both traditional and exotic Jewish breads. Keep perusing, because there are also many recipes included of tasty, healthy and unusual breads.

Try it. You will be pleasantly surprised at how easy and satisfying it is to bake challah and bread.

Try it. Your family will be excited by the delicious, enticing aromas wafting out of your kitchen.

Try it. You will be enriched by the experience.

From one homemaker to another, it is my hope and prayer that you will enjoy this book and utilize the techniques and recipes within it for many years to come.

Enjoy!

Tamar Ansh

Blessings for Bread and Cake

WASHING HANDS

Before eating bread, Jewish law requires washing the hands with a ritual washing cup, known in Yiddish as a *neggel vasser* cup. This process, called *netilas yadayim* is done by filling the cup with clean water and pouring it over the right hand from the wrist down two times in succession, then pouring it over the left hand in the same fashion. The *neggel vasser* cup has has two handles, but any large cup may be used. Then the blessing is recited:

BARUCH ATA
ADONOY
ELOHEINU
MELECH
HA-OLAM
ASHER
KEEDSHANU
BE-MITZVOSAV
VETZEEVANU
AL NETILAS
YADAYIM.

בָּרוּךְ אַתָּה יְיָ
אֱלֹהֵינוּ מֶלֶךְ
הָעוֹלָם,
אֲשֶׁר קִדְּשָׁנוּ
בְּמִצְוֹתָיו
וְצִוָּנוּ עַל
נְטִילַת יָדָיִם

BLESSING BEFORE EATING BREAD

After that, hold the bread in both hands and recite the blessing:

BARUCH ATA
ADONOY
ELOHEINU MELECH
HA-OLAM
HA-MOTZI LECHEM
MIN HA-ARETZ.

בָּרוּךְ אַתָּה יְיָ
אֱלֹהֵינוּ מֶלֶךְ
הָעוֹלָם, הַמּוֹצִיא
לֶחֶם מִן הָאָרֶץ

These blessings are made for all the breads in this book EXCEPT those recipes that are clearly marked "*mezonos*", which are considered cake (i.e. most of the recipes in Chapter 8, "fun & differents ideas"). Items whose blessing was questionable were reviewed by a Rabbi in order to determine their proper blessing.

PIZZA

Pizza is an exception to this rule. When eating pizza, if one is planning to eat two slices, the blessing is *ha-motzi*. If one eats less that that, the blessing is mezonos.

BIRKAS HAMAZON

After a meal with bread, the blessing called *birkas ha-mazon* is recited. The text can be found in any Jewish prayer book.

MEZONOS

Those recipes that are *mezonos* do not need ritual washing; one just makes the blessing:

BARUCH ATA ADONOY ELOHEINU MELECH HA-OLAM BOREI MINEI MEZONOS.

בָּרוּךְ אַתָּה יְיָ אֱלֹהֵינוּ מֶלֶךְ הָעוֹלָם, בּוֹרֵא מִינֵי מְזוֹנוֹת

The after blessing for *mezonos* can be found in any Jewish prayer book as well.

Macrocosm and Microcosm

BY REBBETZIN TZIPORAH HELLER

AS CHILDREN WE ALL had a sense of wonder when we observed the world around us. Unfortunately, routine living takes a heavy toll, and the sense of wonder that we all had fades until we reach a point where we look at the world around us and see very little of its beauty or meaning. The vast majority of people who form public opinion in the Western world have little sense of how deep the connection is between the world and its Creator. Avodah Zarah (idol worship) begins when people separate the ultimate gift, reality itself, from the Giver. They devote themselves to aggrandizing (and in earlier times actually worshiping) the design, and losing sight of the Designer of the universe.

Midrash Rabbah (Vayikra 15:6) tells us that "One who keeps the mitzvah of challah is counted as though he has abolished idolatry." The Sfas Emes, one of our great Chassidic rabbis, tells us how: "The mitzvos give each Jew connection to their G-dly Root. Even bread has something within it that comes from on High." This is an entirely different approach than that of the nations who see divisiveness and variation where we see unity.

The way we see the mini-world, ourselves, is also complex. For some people the "I" is only the tangible side of who they are. If you were to ask a fellow passenger on the train to work, "Who are you?" (which is a dangerous idea to begin with), no doubt the answer will fall into this category. For others, the true self is the soul, and the body is viewed as an interloper or enemy who must be battled until it submits to the soul. If you were to ask the fellow that you may have observed in National Geographic hanging by his ankles deep in meditation, this is the answer he would give you.

The Judaic view is that both the body and the soul are gifts, and both must be nurtured. They are part of one whole, just as the dough from which bread is made is neither water (which is sometimes used as an allegory for the soul) nor flour (which is sometimes used as an allegory for the body) alone, but an indivisible mixture. The entire mixture is uplifted when a blessing is said and challah is taken.

The effect is using the material world in a way in which its latent spirituality is awakened. We are using the gift to reach the Giver, using our bodies to uplift our souls. Whenever we do the mitzvah of separating challah, we redefine ourselves and redefine the world. Its taste, fragrance, and the delight of baking are a joy to the body and to the soul.

This book will enhance your pleasure and nurture your spirit. Enjoy!

Rebbetzin Tziporah Heller is a renowned speaker and Senior Lecturer at Neve Yerushalayim College for Women in Jerusalem, Israel. She is the author of *More Precious Than Pearls, This Way Up!,* and *Our Bodies, Our Souls* (Feldheim Publishers).

Foreword

BY REBBETZIN SARAH MEISELS

(Daughter of R' Shlomo Halberstam, zt"l, the Bobover Rebbe, Kiryat Bobov, Bat Yam, Israel)

IT IS WRITTEN in Yechezkel (44:30),
"וראשית עריסתיכם תתנו לכהן להניח ברכה אל ביתך".
"And the first of your [dough] you should give to the Kohein, in order that blessing will rest in your home."

Taking challah is one of the sources of strengthening our emunah, as the Sefer HaChinuch explains. By enforcing and strengthening our emunah, we merit the zechus of having Hashem Yisborach place a brachah in our households — literally — as the verse says, "להניח ברכה אל ביתך".

Interestingly as well, it is from this particular verse that Chazal teach us that the vehicle for the household's brachah is through the woman — the one who bakes the challah.

How happy we should all be by knowing that while we are separating challah, we are correcting the sin of Chavah and by doing this, we are also actually generating a continuous flow of all kinds of brachos!

Is there a greater thing we can do for our families than to prepare for Shabbos Kodesh with the great mitzvah of hafrashas challah — the very mitzvah that brings blessing into our homes?

In the merit of this great mitzvah of challah, may we all merit to see many yeshuos. Hafrashas challah is a time of bakashah, a time to request and beseech Hashem from the depths of our hearts. It is an eis ratzon, a special time before Him for our prayers to be readily accepted in Shamayim, in Heaven.

ויהי רצון שימלא ד' כל משאלות לבנו לטובה.

אשרינו שזכינו
How fortunate are we that we merit to perform such a vital and great mitzvah.

בברכת כל טוב
Sarah Meisels

Challah – The Universal Mitzvah

IN WELCOMING THE PUBLICATION of a book on the mitzvah of challah by Tamar Ansh, I sincerely pray that this work will inspire more and more women to take advantage of the Heavenly blessings which are bestowed upon those who separate and bake challah.

As opposed to tithing, which applies only in Eretz Yisrael, challah is a universal mitzvah that Jewish women can fulfill everywhere .

Baking challahs for Shabbos and Yom Tov has always been a special custom that has enriched these holy days.

Taking challah is a mitzvah for everyone, but is traditionally the role of the woman, and it is to her that this book is directed. Much has been written in our sacred sources about the impact of this mitzvah on the spiritual state of the woman and the blessings it brings to her household.

May this book, which will teach women how to both "take and bake" challah, be a source of blessing for all who read and use it.

Rav Mendel Weinbach
Founder and Dean,
Yeshivas Ohr Somayach

At Ohr Somayach/Tanenbaum College in Jerusalem, students explore their heritage under the guidance of today's top Jewish educators. For information, please write to info@ohr.edu or visit www.ohr.edu

Chapter 1

Picture-Perfect Challah Tips

Picture-Perfect Challah Tips

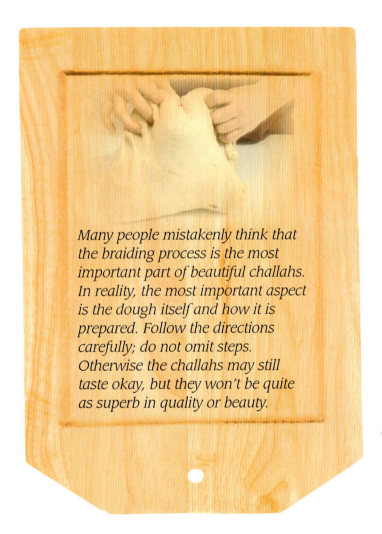

Many people mistakenly think that the braiding process is the most important part of beautiful challahs. In reality, the most important aspect is the dough itself and how it is prepared. Follow the directions carefully; do not omit steps. Otherwise the challahs may still taste okay, but they won't be quite as superb in quality or beauty.

The first time you make challah should NOT be at a time that is pressured or limited, such as on Friday afternoon or the day before a major holiday. Leave yourself time to be more relaxed about it. This way you will be able to concentrate, enjoy, and do a proper job.

From start to finish, challahs ideally take a total of 4-6 hours of time. There is the dough-making, shaping, rising, and baking, as well as cooling down, bagging and freezing the breads properly.
All these steps are equally important.

If you do not bag and freeze your breads properly, they won't taste fresh when served. It is vital to take care of this last step so all your hard and beautiful work will not go to waste.

However, that being said, you shouldn't feel tied down to doing only challah during all this time. You can certainly do all sorts of other things in between these steps, just by utilizing the time efficiently.

Practice the braiding techniques with Play-dough a few days BEFORE you want to make these new shapes. This will improve your challah-making skills immensely. Once you've practiced enough to feel confident with the various shaping ideas, you will then have a much easier time when shaping with real dough.

Remember that one shouldn't expect perfection on the first or second try. Perfecting a challah technique takes time; keep trying, and over time, your technique — and your challahs — will keep improving.

Cover raw challahs loosely with cut plastic tablecloths or the like, when they are rising. The plastic keeps the challah dough from drying out and also helps the rising process.

Make the strands of dough by first rolling out each piece with a rolling pin and then rolling up the flattened dough by hand (as will be delineated below). This method makes a tremendous difference in how professional your challahs will look, rise, and taste. It does take extra time—but it is well worth it.

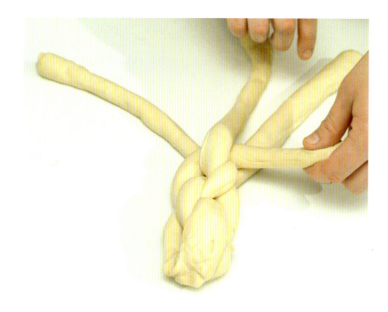

Use parchment baking paper. In Israel, this is called *niyar afiyah*. In the United States, this is NOT wax paper. Wax paper smokes when it's being baked and doesn't work as well. Parchment baking paper often comes in long rolls in the Unites States, and can be cut to size.

More Tips and Notes

YEAST NOTES

For exact yeast conversion measurements, please see the Measurements and Conversions section at the end of the book (pages 200-201).

From both my experience and my research among other bakers, a cube or packet of fresh yeast granules that is **50 grams,** will generally translate into use as **2 ounces of fresh yeast.** Two ounces is 56.70 grams. But for our purposes, since in Israel and other countries fresh yeast often comes

in 50-gram packets, this adaptation works perfectly fine.

To translate that into dry yeast, 50 grams of fresh yeast would be 2 T. plus ¾ tsp. of dry yeast (this is also equivalent to 6¾ tsp.). In other words, a bit more than 2 T. of dry yeast.

EGG GLAZE NOTES

For regular bread loaves or small challahs *only*, if there is a preference not to brush the bread with egg, there are other ways to maintain that shiny look and moisture without the extra egg glaze. When preheating the oven, fill an oven tray with several inches of water and leave it on the bottommost rack of your oven. This will add humidity to the oven, and when the bread is

baking, that moisture will help to form a beautiful crust that will still be moist and delicious, even without the brushed egg on it. If you would like to add seeds to the top of your bread without using an egg glaze, simply fill an empty, clean spray bottle with water, spray your risen dough gently with it, and sprinkle on the seeds of your choice while the dough is still moist. Then proceed to bake with the water tray in the bottom of the oven as described above.

*And last, but not least, to really ensure beautiful challahs, it always pays to say a small prayer for success in your efforts first, asking G-d to make sure they will come out excellent. Then you are **really** ready to start!*

Seven Steps to Amazing Challah

STEP ONE: *Setting Up Your Workspace*

Making challah is really a very simple, uncomplicated procedure, and does not require fancy or confusing equipment. However, it does help if you have the following items:

Before you begin, *make sure you have all the ingredients, fresh and ready, the day* **before** *you want to make your challahs.*

The ingredients needed are:

- canola oil
- fresh yeast
- sugar
- salt
- warm water
- an adequate amount of flour
- parchment baking paper
- good quality freezer bags

(NOT nylon; the bags should be heavy freezer-proof plastic)

Then, *ideally the night before, clear your kitchen and work area so there is plenty of uncluttered, free space in which to work. This will both relax you and give you the room to lay everything out without becoming overwhelmed.*

Loaf Pans

Baking Trays, Parchment Baking Paper

A Sharp (*pareve*) Knife for slicing the dough

Rolling Pin
– *a must.*

Measuring
Cups

Measuring
Beakers

Dough Hook
for Mixer

Measuring
Spoon

A Proper Pastry Brush,
with very fine real hairs.
*If you attempt to use a brush with
coarse or plastic/nylon bristles, the
bristles may pop your risen challahs
and they will deflate before they
have baked.*

STEP TWO: Making the Dough

Sift the flour.[1] *This can be done the night before and placed in a large garbage bag to save time, although you can certainly sift the flour the same day you plan to make the dough. Close the bag tightly until ready for use.*

Boil a few cups of water. In one small *pareve* bowl or measuring cup, put ½ cup boiling water and 1 cup tap water together. Test with your finger to make sure it is very warm *but not boiling. Water that is too hot kills the yeast activity.*

Add ¼ cup of the sugar to this water and then the fresh yeast. Cover this small bowl with a plate and set it aside for 10 minutes to make sure the yeast starts bubbling. *This means the yeast is activating. If the yeast doesn't bubble, it means the yeast is not good; discard, and start again.*

In a large mixer bowl (*if you don't have a mixer you can certainly do this by hand*) place in this order:[2]
- oil • the rest of the sugar
- 2 cups warm water
- salt • 8 cups flour

[1] *Sifting flour has two purposes. For baking purposes, it makes the flour lighter and more airy. For our purposes, it removes small bugs and their larvae from the flour. For foods to be kosher, all bugs must be removed. In Israel, sifting the flour with a fine mesh sieve is an imperative step. In other countries, ask your local rabbi. Make sure to state what kind of flour you are using.*

Mix all very well until a thin sort of batter forms. After the yeast mixture has bubbled,

add this also and mix again.

Now start adding the remaining flour slowly, one or two cups at a time, until it is all mixed in.

[2] Salt and yeast should not be added near each other as they "don't get along well" together. That is why the salt was added after all else here, right before the flour.

By this point, all of the ingredients except for the remaining water should be mixed in. The total amount of water used so far is about 4 cups.

Keep adding a quarter cup of water at a time to the dough until a pliable, smooth, and non-sticky consistency is reached.

If the dough is too firm, you need to add a bit more water and also 2 more tablespoons of oil. If the dough is too soft or wet, add a bit more flour, even if you have to go over the 17-cup limit somewhat. In general, you will use a total of about 5 cups of water. *Climates, different flours, and different yeasts all make a vast difference in this stage.*

Grease your hands or a large plastic spatula with a fine layer of oil. Scrape

down the sides of the bowl and mix the dough at the very bottom of the bowl to insure that all the flour is well mixed into your dough,

and that it is uniform in texture all around. If there is excess flour on the bottom of the bowl, you may need to add a bit more oil to the bottom of the bowl before remixing. Use a little oil rather than water in order to keep the dough from becoming too sticky.

IN GENERAL, in order to keep your dough pliable, non-sticky, and smooth, use small amounts of oil on the outside of the dough, NOT extra flour. Too much flour dries out the dough in the long run, whereas the fine layer of oil keeps it from sticking and makes it easier to work with, helps it rise better, and enhances its overall taste.

There are two kinds of fresh yeast.

One is in cube form,

one is in granules.

Both are sold in the refrigerator section of the supermarket. Check the dates on them to make sure they are fresh. This kind of yeast is preferable for both quality and taste.

For challahs, I usually use only the cubes.

For yeast cakes, I use either, but more often I use the granules.

STEP THREE: The First Rising

Cover the bowl with the dough inside — do not remove it from the mixer yet — and let it rise in the bowl for 10 minutes.

Uncover and knead, with a drop more oil, for another 5 minutes.

For added smoothness, you can cover the dough one more time for 10 minutes, and then knead by hand the final time for another 5 minutes until smooth and workable. Just look at how much nicer that same messy, ugly dough appears now!

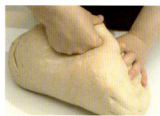

Grease your hands lightly and remove the dough from the mixing bowl.

At this point, it is appropriate to do the mitzvah of "separating challah", if your dough is large enough. See the laws of Separating Challah on pages 187-199 at the end of this book.

If you are not shaping challahs until later on in the day, or if you chose to make the dough at night in order to shape and bake it the next morning, place the dough in a very large garbage bag and remove all the air from the bag. Tie the ends of the bag together, giving the dough plenty of space to rise, and place the bag in the refrigerator. Remove from the refrigerator 30–45 minutes before you want to be ready to shape the challahs.

If you are shaping right away, leave the dough in the garbage bag, or covered well with plastic, on the counter for 1 hour before shaping. It will rise at least double in size. No

extra flour is needed at this point!

Now you are ready to shape the dough. Prepare

your hands, as well as your working surface, by coating them with a very small amount of oil.

VERY IMPORTANT TIP:

In order for the dough to rise properly after it is shaped, it's imperative that you punch it down now and re-knead it for 2-4 minutes. Following this "punching down" step will ensure that the strands of dough won't overstretch and break while rising and baking. It also allows the trapped gases inside the dough to be released, and then the shaped breads rise as they should.

To do this, literally punch down the dough and then turn it out onto your working surface. Continue to punch and knead it by turning it over and over for another 2-4 minutes. Then **stop kneading.** *It is no longer necessary to knead it anymore. Over-kneading it can over-activate it, and make it difficult to shape later.*

STEP FOUR: *Preparing the Baking Trays*

Prepare the baking trays by taking out about five of them and lining them with parchment baking paper.

The parchment baking paper will stay in place on the tray if you first squirt a bit of water on the tray, and then immediately lay the paper on top of the water. Your tray will also stay cleaner this way, both because there is no oil on the tray and also because the paper keeps the tray free of dough.

STEP FIVE: Shaping the Dough

Now we are ready to shape the dough! On the following pages you will find step-by-step instructions for many different kinds of traditional challahs. You may pick and choose from each of the sizes and techniques that suit your baking style and your family's needs.

SHAPING STEP 1:

Cut off slices of dough and, with the aid of your rolling pin, roll each one out to a medium-thin

oval. It should not be too thin, or it will break, nor too thick, or it won't roll properly. Starting from the top of your rolled-out piece, now roll it towards you, so it resembles a rolled-up log.

Make about 10–12 of such logs and set them off to the side of your working surface.

Cover them loosely with a disposable plastic tablecloth so they will not dry out, and let them rise for 5 minutes. They will appear somewhat blown up and smoother once risen.

SHAPING STEP 2:
Roll out each strand gently before attempting to work with it. This will give your strands a smooth, professional appearance, will make them longer and easier to work with, and will decrease the look of the "seam" that was created by making it into a roll previously. When rolling each one out, keep your hands lightly greased, and work from the center, rolling gently with both hands, outwards.

If you want your challahs to appear higher in their center, and lower at the edges, then you should slightly increase the pressure on the roll as you work outwards so the roll will appear somewhat fatter in the center, and thinner at the ends.

SHAPING STEP 3:
Choose which shape of challah you would like to work with from the pages that follow, and shape your challahs.

After challahs are shaped, allow them to rise for 45 minutes on the baking trays, with plenty of room between them since they will grow tremendously.

Very important note!
Do not let the challahs over-rise. When challahs over-rise, they become too light and airy, and later on, when they are glazed with egg they often burst and fall flat. Other times, although they may hold their shape after being egged, the braids may split and come apart in the oven while baking.

Cover them loosely with plastic while they rise so they will remain moist and plump. It's usually best to keep the same size challahs on each sheet; these pictures of raw challahs demonstrate the different kinds of challahs as they rise.

STEP SIX: Now You're Ready to Bake

The following are your baking instructions for all regular challahs. This applies to every shape of regular challah.

PREHEAT THE OVEN TO 375°F/190°C FOR 20 MINUTES PRIOR TO BAKING!! Make an egg mixture (known as an egg glaze) of 2 whole eggs plus 1 egg yolk and one tsp. oil. Mix together and brush gently over the risen challahs.

NOTE: The type of brush you use is vital. Use one with soft, real hairs. Real paint brushes or professional baker's brushes are great for this. The ones with plastic or hard nylon hairs may cause your challahs to burst and fall before they are even baked.

If you want to add any **toppings** to your challahs, such as poppy seeds, sesame seeds, or cinnamon and sugar, now is the time.

For large challahs, bake 20–25 minutes until the challahs start to turn brown.

Lower the heat to 350°F/180°C and continue baking until challahs are done, when they are browned completely on the bottom also.

*Larger challahs usually take **at least** another 25–30 minutes, often more, on the lower temperature. Smaller rolls take less time. Size and shapes of challah, climate, and oven types and sizes all make a difference.*

For small challah rolls, baking time is far less: 10 minutes on the higher temperature, 10–15 minutes on the lower temperature. This means about 20 minutes *total baking time.*

Always check the bottoms of the challahs before removing from the oven, making sure that they are a nice brown color and firm texture. This means your challahs are done.

Freeze airtight as described on the following page.

STEP SEVEN: Cooling, Bagging & Serving

At the end of your baking session, leave the challahs on a wire rack to cool off, so they will not become soft and wet from their own steam as they cool.

Then, to insure same-day freshness at all times, bag each one properly in good quality, heavy-duty freezer bags.

Remove the air from the bags, seal tightly shut by tying a firm knot or securely taping it closed with tape, and place in your deep freezer immediately.

To serve, simply remove from the freezer several hours before you wish to serve it and let it defrost.

If you like the idea of warm, fresh-from-the-oven challah, place your challahs on top of a hot pot on the blech* for about an hour before eating. Throw a cloth over the challah's top, but don't wrap it tightly or completely. They will be warm, steamy, and simply scrumptious when you slice them open. Alternatively, one can wrap the challahs loosely with foil and place them in a warm oven with the heat turned off. Remove them from the oven directly before Kiddush and place on the challah tray. Delicious!

* Once Shabbos has commenced, one cannot place challahs (nor any food or pot for that matter) directly onto a fire. Religious Jews use a "blech" instead to keep food hot during Shabbos. This is a special flat hotplate with only one temperature or a special metal piece put over a small flame on the stovetop that keeps the food hot but does not actually cook the food. When warming up a challah on Shabbos, people place them on top of a hot pot that is already on the blech from before Shabbos started.

Patience and Growth

IT TOOK ME a few weeks of marriage, and the constant nudging of my husband, to finally get me to try to make challahs on my own. In fact, in the beginning I really only did them because he drove me crazy about it. I knew that my mother made good challah, but she was on the other side of the globe, and besides, I couldn't seem to make heads or tails of her recipe. So I started to search around for a recipe I could do and would also like.

Since I was "going it alone" without a good book on challah (like this one!) and without anyone to really ask, I started trying recipes on my own. None seemed to work well. I also used to come home late from my office job and had hardly any time for baking, so I would dutifully make the dough, then shape it, and bake it without waiting for it to rise at all. I did not realize that in order for challahs to be really good, one has to have the patience for them to rise. But patience was a commodity I possessed little of, especially in those years. When I think back now to those early years of challah baking, I cringe internally. They were so awful! And whatever guests we had would politely chew and swallow them anyhow. Who knows how many stomachaches I caused in those days. And my challahs themselves? They were the ugliest things on the face of this earth.

Thank G-d, I've learned a measure of patience and understanding since then, and it is certainly reflected in my challahs. I can now look back and see my challah-baking experiences in a new light; that of growth and maturity, one that was gained only by trial and error, only by the passage of time and age.

Chapter 3

Large Challah Shapes

Basic Three-Braided Challah

Take three strands of rolled-out dough and pinch them together at one end.

Take one of the outer strands and move it over the center strand.

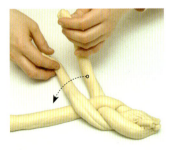

Then take the other strand on the opposite side of the challah and put that one over the center strand.

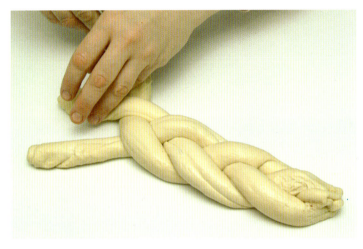

Keep braiding in this fashion by constantly going from one outer edge strand to the next, and bringing the strands towards the center each time.

When done, pinch the ends together and tuck underneath somewhat. Lay them side by side on your lined baking trays, with plenty of space to rise at least double in all directions.

To create a loaf-shaped challah, line a loaf pan with a strip of parchment baking paper and place the challah inside.

This size dough will create a challah this shape, basically this size.

Standard Four-Braided Challah

Take four strands of rolled-out dough and pinch them together at one end. Lay out the strands in front of you and count them from left to right, by numbering them as 1,2,3,4.

[**A**] Take strand 2 and place it, going towards the right, over towards the far right end.

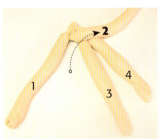

[**B**] Take strand 1 and pull it over the stump of where 2 was pinched at the top, and into the center of the strands, i.e., between 3 and 4.

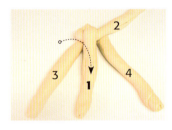

Now reverse the order. Look at the strands in front of you going in the opposite direction, from **right to left**, and label them 1,2,3 and 4.

[**C**] Repeat the same technique as you did previously.

What is now 2, place over and to the far left on top.

[**D**] what is now 1, should go over the bump on top and be placed in the center, between 3 and 4.

Now reverse the process again and do it the way you did the first time. Keep going with this pattern, from one side of the challah to the other, until the strands are too short to be braided any further.

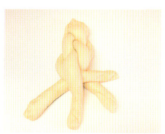

Pinch the last bits of dough together and tuck them under the challah. Shape gently with your lightly greased hands until the challah looks like this:

Leave to rise, covered loosely with plastic, for about an hour.

This is how my daughter's looked after it rose.

A Rabbi's Blessing

AFTER SEVERAL YEARS of marriage and our dreams of children in the home still unrealized, my husband once brought up our situation to a certain rabbi. The very first thing this rabbi asked him was, "Does your wife bake challah for Shabbos?" My husband answered in the affirmative, because I had indeed been making challah since the beginning of our marriage. Somehow the rabbi thought to ask further. "But does your wife make enough dough to actually do the mitzvah of challah, the mitzvah called **hafrashas challah**? [For further clarification, see the Halachos of Separating Challah section at the end of this book.]

I had deliberately, all those years, not made enough dough to perform the mitzvah properly, as I didn't know the laws of challah and was afraid to "do it wrong." So, instead, I simply made only a small amount at once, thereby circumventing the entire mitzvah.

When my husband told the rabbi that no, I did not take challah with a blessing, the first thing the rabbi told him was to go home and promptly encourage me to make the full amount of dough, thereby warranting a brachah. Because it is from this brachah, this blessing, that the blessings of the home and of children come, and it is one of the Jewish woman's pivotal jobs in the foundation of her home.

The first time I finally did this mitzvah properly, and made the brachah along with some heartfelt prayers, I felt an incredible, special feeling welling up inside of me.

And yes, eventually the rabbi's blessing for children came true as well. It did take some time, but thank G-d, we have several beautiful children today, all of whom, sons included, already know how to make our beautiful challahs ...

Six-Braided Challah

Exactly the same technique that was applied for the Four-Braided Challah will apply now, only there are two extra strands.

Make 6 strands and pinch them together at one end. Lay out the strands in front of you and count them from left to right, numbering them as 1,2,3,4,5 and 6.

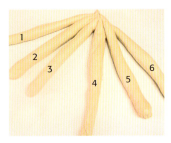

KNOT

First make a knot on top that you will be working from. To do this, take strand 2 and move it up and all the way over to the right.

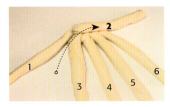

Then take strand 6 over to the far left.

To complete the first knot, take strand 2 (and place it over the bump and down between strands 3 and 4.

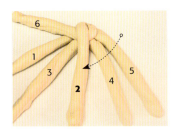

BRAIDING

[A] Re-number the strands from left to right, from 1 to 6.

Take strand 2 and place it, going towards the right, over the far right end.

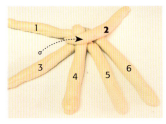

[B] Take strand 1 and place it over the "bump" of the first knot, into the center of the strands – between 4 and 5.

Now reverse the order.
Look at the strands from right to left, and re-label them from 1 to 6.

[C] Follow the same instructions as above, but in the opposite direction. What is now 2, place over and to the far left on top (near the bump that has been created on top by now).

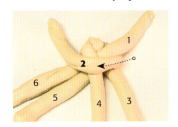

[D] Then take what is now 1, (the one that was sticking out over to the far right make it go over the bump on top and place it in the center, between 4 and 5.

Reverse the process again, by going back to step A and continue through D, repeating A-D until the strands are fully braided.

Pinch the last bits of dough together and tuck them a bit under the challah. Shape gently with your lightly greased hands .

This is how the challah looked once it rose completely and was just about ready to be brushed and baked.

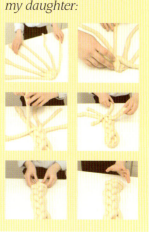

Now let's review the braiding together with my daughter:

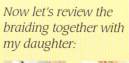

The "Shabbos Tefillin"

THERE IS A FAMOUS STORY about the Brisker Rav, HaRav Yitzchok Zev Soloveitchik (1886–1959). He was one of the leading rabbis of prewar Europe, and he felt very strongly about the importance of a woman's challah baking.

There was a lovely family living near the Rav who had two teenaged daughters. Every Friday morning, the mother would wake up especially early, in order to begin her preparations for making the dough for their challahs. In those days, no one had private ovens in their homes. Rather, each family would prepare their own challahs, lay them carefully in their own trays, and then march off to the communal bakery where they would be baked in the bakery's oven by the baker of that area. The baker would tell each family what time to return for their freshly baked breads, and each took care to come back when he told them. After all, no one wanted their hard work to go to waste or to get lost in the busy bakery on Friday afternoon.

Every Friday morning, the mother, Mrs. "Katz," woke up her two eldest daughters early. "Come girls," she said. "Please get up right now. The day is short and the challahs have yet to be shaped and baked."

That did it. The girls didn't want to miss out on the special time of kneading, shaping, and baking challah with their mother. As the two girls busied themselves with their morning wake-up routine, Mrs. Katz was already in the kitchen, starting to sift her flour and prepare the ingredients.

Slowly, carefully, and with dedication, the three of them worked at the dough, kneading it gently, letting it rise. Then came the special moment when their mother separated the challah, and her heartfelt prayers could be heard, murmured softly amid the hum of the kitchen's activity. Only then did the real fun of shaping begin. Before they all knew it, the challahs were all shaped, neatly lined up one next to the other, pristinely awaiting their turn in the communal bakery's oven.

Both girls carefully lifted the trays, and together strode off to the bakery. Each week they passed by Rav Soloveitchik's study window, carrying their Shabbos delicacy, gently, carefully, and with love.

> **"WHEN YOUR DAUGHTERS DID NOT PASS BY MY HOME THIS WEEK WITH THEIR BEAUTIFUL CHALLAHS, I KNEW SOMETHING HAD TO BE WRONG."**

One week, Mrs. Katz attempted to get up early on Friday as she always did. Her challah-dough making awaited her. But she was feeling so awful. Her temperature had risen during the night and now all her strength was gone.

"Please stay in bed and rest," Mr. Katz said to her. "You shouldn't get up before the doctor comes to check you."

"But what will be with my challahs!" she cried. "I have to get moving or they won't be done in time!"

"No matter," he answered her back. "This week we will just have to suffice with store-bought challahs. In the meantime, your health comes first."

That Friday, the girls never passed by the Brisker Rav's window, since they had no challahs of their own to bake.

Friday night after prayers, the Rav motioned to Mr. Katz that he wanted to speak with him. Hurriedly, Mr. Katz approached the Rav.

"I just wanted to make sure that everything is all right in your home," the Rav asked him.

"Well, to be honest, my wife isn't feeling so good," Mr. Katz replied. "But how did the Rav realize that something was amiss?"

"When your daughters did not pass by my home this week with their beautiful challahs, I knew something had to be wrong. I wish your wife a complete recovery and that by next week, you will have home-baked challahs once again at your table." The Rav paused for a bit, a thoughtful look on his face. "You know," he continued, "a woman's challahs are like her 'tefillin'."

"What did the Rav say?" asked Mr. Katz in wonderment.

"A woman's challahs are like her tefillin. Women are not commanded in the mitzvah of tefillin, the mitzvah that is the special Jewish sign, the 'ois,' of Jewish men. So what then is their special sign? That sign is Shabbos itself, since it says about Shabbos: 'Ois hee l'olam'; in other words, it is their sign for generations. The time and energy women put into their Shabbos challahs are their special 'tefillin.'

And, thank G-d, the Brisker Rav's blessing came true, because by the next week Mrs. Katz was completely better, and back to her special challah baking for Shabbos as usual.

Jewish men put on tefillin (phylacteries) every day of the week except for Shabbos. Tefillin are called "ois" in the Torah, meaning they are a sign; a sign between Jews and G-d that we are His Nation. Since Shabbos is the ultimate Sign between G-d and the Jewish People, tefillin are therefore unnecessary on Shabbos and that is why the law is that they are not worn on that day.

Woven Round Challah

Round challahs are most traditionally used for the Jewish New Year, Rosh HaShanah. At the beginning of our new year, to usher in a sweet and delectable judgment, many people have the custom to serve sweetened foods, and challah is no exception to this rule. For this reason, Rosh HaShanah challahs are often sweeter than those served the rest of the year. Some add more sugar than they normally do to the dough, others add raisins to the dough, still others do both. I enjoy adding all this to my challahs, but with another twist too; after they are egg-glazed and ready to be baked, I sprinkle each with a mixture of cinnamon and sugar. The smell they emit while baking is absolutely heavenly, and the taste is out of this world. Truly a holiday treat!

To begin with the shaping of these special challahs, make the strands by rolling out each ball of dough with a rolling pin.

Roll up into logs towards you and set aside for 10 minutes on your work table, under a plastic disposable tablecloth so they won't dry out. They will have risen somewhat.

Take your risen dough strands

and roll them out gently as long as possible.

Do this with four pieces of dough until they are all about the same length. Lay the pieces out in front of you, tic-tac-toe style.

Each strand should be placed in opposite directions; one side is over/under, the next row is then under/over. There should now be 4 sets of 2 strands each coming out from the four sides of the woven middle, one under and one over in each set.

*If you intend to **add raisins** to your Rosh HaShanah challahs, place them all around the flat piece of rolled out dough and roll it up.*

When you go to shape the dough, the raisins will all be well hidden inside and will be delicious when the challah is sliced open.

From each set, pick up the one that was "under" and pull it over its partner, thereby placing each of these "unders" over their corresponding partner, in a counterclockwise rotation.

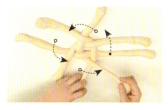

Practically speaking, this means that the *left* piece of each set will be placed *over the right* piece of each set.

When this rotation is done, **work in the opposite direction,** clockwise. What was formerly the right piece, will now go over the left piece in the clockwise direction; the pieces are not yet next to each other as they are still apart from the first rotation; pull them close to each other and bring the right piece, i.e. the one you did not touch in the first rotation, over the left piece of the neighboring strand:

After this second rotation is done, do a third one, now in the other direction.

Do one more opposite rotation if you have enough dough left.

To finish, pinch each set of two ends together firmly, then bring all four sets together towards the center.

Now comes the really fun part: carefully flip over your challah and look!

You now have a beautiful, woven, round challah.

Leave to rise on a large baking tray that has been lined with parchment baking paper. Cover the challahs loosely with disposable plastic tablecloths while rising.

After 20 minutes of rising, turn on your oven to preheat at 400°F / 200°C, as most ovens take 20 minutes to reach full temperature.

After the full 40 minutes of rising time, glaze your challahs and place them directly into the hot oven, for optimum baking results.

Bake for 35-40 minutes until the top and bottom are golden.

Braided Round Challah

Another way to make nice, round, braided challahs is by taking three long strands and braiding them into a very long Havdalah–candle-shaped log.

After this has been braided, carefully tie it up as if you are making one large knot out of it, and leave it to rise. It will come out different than a simple round knot, and although not quite as extravagant as the woven round challah, it is still quite pretty.

Both of these large round challahs work wonderfully well as whole wheat also, as seen on pages 46-47. The lighter challah is only white flour, the darker one is whole wheat.

Simchah Challah

A simchah challah is traditionally a very large challah, the kind most often seen at wedding or circumcision feasts, or for any special occasion where there will be a lot of people at one meal. This is where the name "simchah challah" comes from, since they are most often used for smachot (happy occasions).

There are several different ways to create such a large challah. Size, however, will depend on the oven size available at baking time. European ovens are usually smaller in depth, so they are capable of holding only a smaller-sized simchah challah. In such an oven, a single recipe of the first recipe in this book, "Always Perfect No-Egg Challah," would make two medium-sized simchah challahs. A larger, more American-sized oven (such as a Caloric, Maytag, or General Electric) could hold one large challah from an entire recipe. It is better to start off smaller and be sure the challah will have adequate room in the oven to grow and bake, than to overestimate and have it hit the sides and door, thereby burning and creating a tremendous mess.

The challah featured in the picture above was made in a European-sized oven, using half of the Always Perfect No-Egg Challah recipe on page 30. The only equipment necessary is the largest size tray that will fit your oven and a large sheet of baking paper. Ideas abound as to how to make such a high and large challah. Here are a few ideas to get you started:

IDEA 1: The one in the picture features a large six-braided challah with a medium sized, very long and thin, three-braided challah laid on its top, going down the center spine. To keep it from falling over when rising, toothpicks were inserted, before rising, into the sides to join both challahs together. The toothpicks were removed only *after* baking was completed.

IDEA 2: Make two medium-sized four-braided challahs and lay them side by side on a large baking tray. Then make a long, thin three-braided challah and lay it over the gap between the two bottom layers. Allow this to rise for an hour and then apply an egg glaze and bake.

Make two thin three-braided challahs and place side by side. To get a full 12 pieces of dough, as is traditional in many families, make a six-braided challah and place this over the gap between the two bottom challahs. These techniques work best if you use a large, oval-shaped pan. In the pictures featured here, I only had a square pan to work with, and because of this the challah came out more square looking. Had I used a more oval shaped pan, then the challah would have come out in a more traditional shape.

Use a large, oval-shaped roasting pan. Make sure to line the pan well with baking paper or spray it well with cooking spray. Make one large round challah. Center this in the middle of the roasting pan. Make another four- or six-braided large challah and place this

OVER the round one on the bottom of the pan. The round one will give height to the braided challah, and as they rise it will grow together to create a beautiful *simchah*-sized challah.

Here you can take a look at two three-braided challahs, with a four-braided challah placed over its center.

For all shapes, after the challah has been placed in the pan, check to make sure it has room to grow without falling over the sides. Leave about 2 inches around all sides, as these types of challah will grow tremendously. The

sides of the pan will help to keep it in check and to force it to grow upwards, and higher, as opposed to only outwards and flatter.

After shaping, cover the challah loosely with a large piece of plastic so it will not dry out while rising. Place it in the bottommost rack of your oven. Remove all other racks.

For this challah, I allow it to rise in the oven in which it will bake, and then turn on the heat to bake, since it will rise more during the baking process as well.

With the challah featured here, it rose so much that I turned the oven on to bake it after only 40 minutes of rising. It rose the rest of the way as it began its baking process.

When baking such a large challah, the baking time will obviously differ. Leave the risen challah in the oven; you do not have to preheat the oven.

Simply turn on your oven and, after applying the egg glaze (always use only a real egg glaze for such a large challah) and adding your topping of choice, let the challah bake at 375°F/190°C for 30 minutes, until it starts to turn golden. Then reduce the heat to 350°F/180°C and let it bake for another hour.

If the challah starts to appear too brown on top, cover it loosely with foil, leaving room on the sides for air to escape, and let it finish baking covered. The challah is done when it is firm and dark brown on its bottom.

Remove carefully from the pan and allow it to cool completely on a wire rack.

When cool, wrap well in a heavy-duty garbage bag and freeze until the day of use.

Pull-Apart Challah

*These beautifully shaped challahs have a long history behind them. To many, these are also known as "**yud-beis**" (Hebrew for 12) challahs, since they are comprised of 12 separate rolls that are allowed to rise together as one whole unit. In the time of the Beis haMikdash (the Temple), there was always fresh bread available (no freezer and no bags involved!!) called the **Lechem haPanim**. Each week, twelve **Lechem haPanim** were baked fresh and they were placed on the Shulchan (table) in the Beis haMikdash.*

Furthermore, each week they miraculously stayed completely fresh until the Kohanim ate them.

There are many methods, ideas, and shapes of how to best make these special challahs. For this book, this is the method I used ...

INGREDIENTS:
- *challah dough*
- *round pan*
- *parchment baking paper*
- *egg glaze*

This picture features a challah baked in a 9-inch round pie pan. You may use any size, but keep in mind that if the pan is much larger than this, you will need a bigger piece of dough.

Cut off a large piece of dough, the same size you would use for a larger six-braided challah. Divide the dough into 11 equal portions, and one larger portion, equaling 12 pieces in all. Roll the larger portion into a round ball and place in the center of the lined pan.

Alternatively, you may shape the center piece as seen here by rolling out the dough into a fat, medium-sized strip and then curling it up like a pinwheel. Place this into the center of the pan.
Continue with all the rest of the pieces of dough in the same manner, either rolling them into plain balls or making pinwheels out of each of them. Place them around the center piece to form a round wheel of dough pieces.
The pieces don't need to touch each other, they will grow together as they rise.

Allow it to rise, covered with a piece of plastic, for 45 minutes. Preheat the oven to 350°F/180°C, about 20 minutes into the rising time. Brush the risen challah with an egg glaze and bake until golden brown on top and bottom, about 40–45 minutes. Remove from the pan and cool on a wire rack.

A Wife's Vow

FOR THE FIRST ten years of my marriage, it never crossed my mind to bake my own challahs. I felt

SARAH'S STORY: that I had "better" things to do with my time, and was sure that baking challahs, which was to me — at least then — a very time-consuming process, was not one of them. So every week I would send my husband to the local Jewish bakery to buy the few challahs we would need for that Shabbos.

One week, my husband went out as usual, late at night close to closing time, to get our challahs. There was a howling snowstorm outside and the roads were becoming slippery and icy. I was a bit nervous, but reminded myself that he had been doing this for years already and this was life in our (then) small Jewish town. Anyhow, there were only two kosher bakeries and they were both the same distance away. I figured, going out Thursday night was sure better than the hassle of the bakery on Friday afternoon.

Well, an hour went by, and then two, and he still did not return. On a normal night it was only a ten-minute drive away from our house. Add to that about a half hour to wait in line, and then a bit more since my husband tends to "shmooze" a lot with other people, and an hour isn't too unusual for him to be gone. But two or three hours??? This was way before cell phones were invented and I started to worry. When more than three hours had gone by, I was almost ready to call the police. Finally, finally, when it was already well after midnight, I heard the garage door open and he came into the house.

AN HOUR WENT BY, AND THEN TWO, AND HE STILL DID NOT RETURN

I was so relieved that I started crying. Then anger took over and I demanded to know what had happened.

My good-hearted husband did dutifully buy me our challahs. However, traffic was so bad at the intersection near the bakery, and the cars there needed assistance, so he did the "good citizen" thing and got out of his own car, into the freezing cold and blinding snow, and stood there directing traffic for a few hours until the police finally showed up.

After that experience, I vowed to myself that I would never send him out Thursday night to buy challahs again! It's been more than 25 years since then, and I've kept that vow ever since.

Bread Basket

This idea was created and executed here by Rochel Baumgarten.

Use any challah dough, white or whole wheat. This picture features a basket made out of white challah dough.

EQUIPMENT:
- *1 disposable pot, 8–10-inch (24–26 cm) round, 10 inches (25 cm) deep*
- *sharp knife*
- *rolling pin*
- *baking tray*

In order to make the braiding of the basket easier, it's a good idea to put the pot you are working with on top of a large bucket, so that it is raised off of your working surface.

Also remember to preheat the oven now to 350°F/180°C, since you will NOT be letting this basket rise before it bakes. As soon as you are done preparing it, you will be baking it.

Roll out a piece of dough into a circle, 1 inch (2.5 cm) thick, large enough to generously cover the entire bottom of the pot. Using a sharp knife, trim the edges so that the dough is more or less even all the way around, while still hanging down over the edges of the pot.

Take another large piece of dough and roll it out into a rectangle, 1.5 inch/ 3¾ cm thick.

Using the sharp knife, cut long strips about 1 inch/ 2.5 cm wide out of this piece of dough. Slit these strips in half.

Attach these strips to the round piece of dough already on the pot, keeping them close together. Do this all the way around the pot until it is completely covered. Let them hang down over the edge of the pot.

Take one very long strip of dough and attach it underneath the strips of dough hanging down by pinching it gently to the underside of one strip. Begin to weave it in and out.

When you get to the end of this weave, attach it again underneath a strip.

If it happens that you suddenly realize in the middle of weaving that your strip of dough won't make it all the way around the pot, simply cut off another strip, pinch them together and tuck it under a weave, and continue weaving as before.

To end the first weave, simply pinch it under one of the strips.

Take another long strip of dough and wrap it around the base of the basket to make it complete, and to hold the weave in place.

Try to end off and begin new weaves at the same area of the basket.

This way when you display it, you can show the front

area where it shows only weave and looks best, and this pinched area, which will look less nice, will be less noticeable.

Continue with the next strip of dough as before.

In this manner you will continue weaving until the whole basket is completed.

You will now be left with strips of dough

hanging down unevenly all around the base of the basket.

Take the sharp knife and trim the basket all the way around. Ideally you should leave about half an inch (1 cm) of dough hanging down since the strips tend to shrink into themselves a bit once they are cut.

This base will later become the upper rim of your basket. ▶

Place the basket, pot and all, onto a lined baking sheet. Brush the basket with egg to glaze it.

To make a handle for use later on, roll out three thin strands of dough, and braid as for a three-braided challah. Make it very long and thin. Curve it around the base of the basket, about halfway around the perimeter of the basket, brush it with egg, and allow it to bake together this way.

Just keep in mind that this handle will in no way be strong enough to actually carry the basket with! Also remember that any time you lift this bread basket you must always support it from the bottom.

After it is baked, let it cool off for 10 minutes and then gently cut the handle off the base with a long sharp knife. Attach it with toothpicks to the sides of the basket to create a handle effect.

Let the basket bake as is until it is golden brown. Remove it from the oven and allow it to cool before gently turning it over and removing the disposable pot.

Use your imagination to fill your basket and present it beautifully. It's a great way to surprise friends and guests, when it is filled with other small rolls or even …with beautiful and colorful fruits in season!

BREAD BOWL
Another idea similar to this one is to make a bread bowl. Take a medium sized metal bowl, and lightly grease it all over on its outside perimeter. Wrap a long roll of dough around it and bake at 350˚F / 180˚C on a lined baking tray until it is golden brown. Allow to cool on a wire rack for 15-20 minutes. Gently loosen it with a sharp knife to release it from the metal bowl. After it is completely cooled, wrap in a large plastic bag and freeze until use.

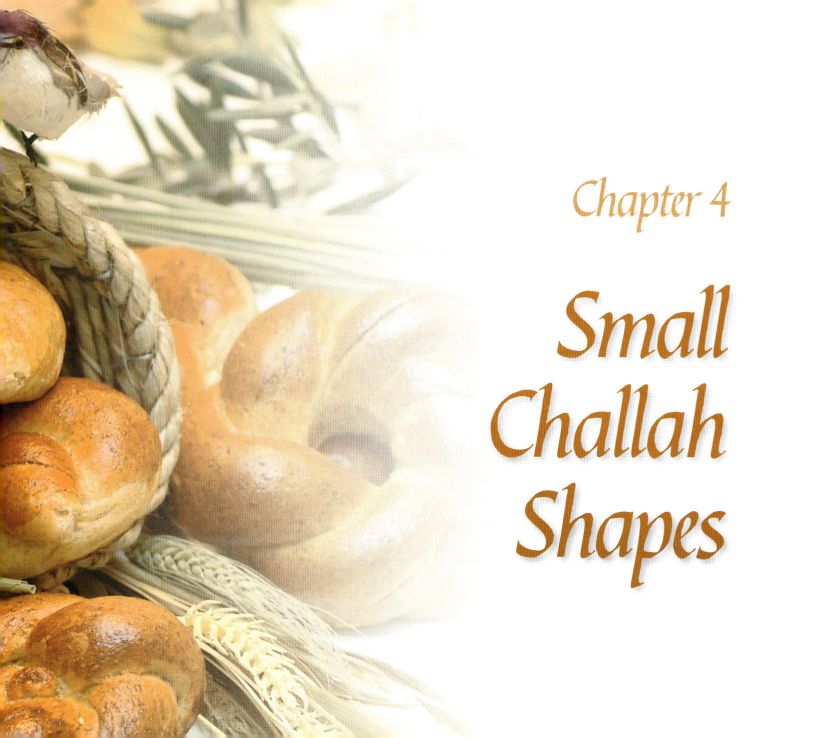

Chapter 4

Small Challah Shapes

Flower-Shaped Challah Roll

The next five roll shapes were all done using only one strand of dough.

For each one, begin by rolling out a long, thin piece of dough. Make a small circle on one end, leaving more than half of the strand out of the circle.

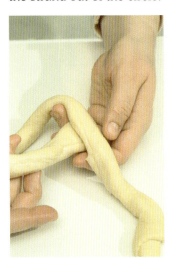

Take the longer end, and place it into the hole and over the side of the small circle three times.

[1] CLOSED FLOWER
pinch the dough closed on the underside and let rise as is.

[2] REAL FLOWER
pull up the last end through the hole and leave it poking up.

Napkin Ring

Make a closed flower roll, as seen on previous page.

Then take a piece of aluminum foil and shape it into a circle.

Place it on the lined baking tray and bake it with this aluminum or metal ring in its center; after it is done baking and it is cool, remove it from the challah's center.

(Alternatively, you can use a metal ring or small cone, if you have them, greasing them well on the outside.) Place this into the center of the unbaked flower roll.

To serve, position a decorative paper napkin in the center of each challah "napkin ring" roll. Place in the center of each person's plate before the guests arrive. This makes a stunning and unique presentation for any festive meal and is sure to bring you loads of compliments!

Knot-Shaped Challah

[4] TRI-CIRCLED LOOK
Take a strand of dough and shape it to resemble the Hebrew letter *ayin*.

Take the side that is under, and tuck it over and into the center of the roll.

Take the other side and tuck it under the opposite side and bring it to the center of the hole. Then pinch both sides where they meet under the roll.

[5] REGULAR ROUND "KNOT"
Take one strand of dough, roll it out and simply knot it once, pulling the end up and through the hole.

Clover Leaf Rolls

Spray a muffin tray or two with baking spray.

Roll out three small rounds of dough.

Place them near each other in each muffin cup.

Cover the muffin tray with plastic and allow the dough to rise until double in size, about 40 minutes.

Smear each roll gently with egg for glazing, and add on any toppings of choice. Bake at 350°F/ 180°C for 20 minutes or until the rolls are uniformly light golden brown.

To make this sweet looking shape, use any challah or bread dough that you would like to make into individual small rolls.

This is a very nice, different looking kind of roll, instead of the typical ordinary round rolls.

Emma Sass's Story

I HAD BEEN FRIENDLY with Jeanne for nearly 10 years. She knew how badly I wanted to be married, and, as my mentor and dear, dear, friend, she listened to me for hours on end, bemoaning my situation and crying buckets. I had been in the dating scene for about nine years already. I was 33 years old and very sad to still be single.

I went on one awful date after another, rarely agreeing to a second date. If I did, the guy would finish it by the third. "Why can't I get anywhere at all?" I would ask Jeanne, time and again.

"Because Hashem is protecting you," she said. "You have such clarity that you know straight away when somebody is not for you."

"Thank Hashem for that," I thought to myself. Of course Jeanne was right, but I still kept crying and wondering what was wrong with me.

What was fantastic about Jeanne (and still is), was that she was probably the only individual left who completely believed I would get married one day, never offering judgmental words or unhelpful dating "hints."

One Friday afternoon, she called me as I was about to face another lonely Shabbos. Her voice — always so bright and chirpy — put a smile on my face as usual. "I just wanted you to know that I organized 40 women to make challah, separating it with a brachah, all on the same day, as a segulah for you to get married. It took place this morning." Not really believing in such things, but feeling so grateful for a friend who cared as much as she did, I replied, "Thank you so much; that's so nice."

I thought nothing of it, until, a week and a half later. I went on a date with someone who was so happy, so full of joy, so full of everything that reminded me of Jeanne and who, just ten weeks later, proposed to me ...

"I always knew that G-d would help you get married," Jeanne said, a few months after our wedding. "Mr. Right just had to be out there. Since G-d created you, then it had to be that your soulmate existed, too."

We have now, thank G-d, been happily married for nearly a year, but I will never forget those dark moments of my loneliness and I am always sympathetic to the plight of my single friends.

And I will forever be grateful to my special friend, Jeanne, who with her heart and even with her challahs, showed me what it truly means to care.

Small Twisted Challah

Take one strand of dough and roll it out to an even thinness and place it in front of you as an "S" shape.

Then take the top part of the "S" and go under the middle point, and lay it towards the left side. Take the bottom part of the "S" and twist it over and towards the right side of the bottom half of the strand.

The bottom strand should now go under the middle point and up through the top hole.

The top strand should now go over the middle point and under through the bottom hole. Voila!

Miracle Challahs

In the Gemara tractate Ta'anis 24b, there is a famous story about the challahs of Rabbi Chanina ben Dosa's wife.

RABBI CHANINA BEN DOSA was one of the great rabbis. He is quoted often in the Gemara. He was a great scholar, and lived a happy life, but a very poverty-stricken one, together with his wife and children. They made do with whatever they had, no matter how little it was. It often happened that there was no food in his house.

One Friday morning, as all the other neighboring homes had smoke coming from their chimneys from all the foods and challahs they were making. Rabbi Chanina's wife got up early to prepare her home for Shabbos and to cook whatever she could. That week, though, there was no money for anything, and certainly not for flour and eggs. Rabbi Chanina's wife was a great woman and she refused to bother her husband over such matters. What did bother her, however, was the knowledge that if her oven were bare and cold, the other neighbors would know because no smoke would be coming from her chimney. Then they would denigrate her special, scholarly husband, who could not even support his family with the bare necessities. So she decided to light a fire in her oven with just some plain sticks of firewood, thereby giving the impression that she too was cooking food in honor of the upcoming Shabbos.

One of her neighbors started wondering about all the smoke coming from Rabbi Chanina's chimney. It was known that the family was quite poor and didn't have money for lots of food. This lowly lady decided she would have a peek into the oven next door to be able to expose, once and for all, the terrible poverty that Rabbi Chanina's family had to endure.

She went over to Rabbi Chanina's house and knocked. Rabbi Chanina's wife decided not to open the door, for she knew this neighbor and she did not want her to see her empty oven and thereby disgrace her husband publicly. So she left the kitchen and went into another room.

The horrible neighbor, however, had no bones

about just marching right in, which is precisely what she did. She went straight over to the hot oven and opened it to look inside. To her complete amazement, the oven was filled with freshly baked challahs! The aroma that wafted out of that oven was just indescribable. And when she turned around, there was even more dough on the table, waiting to go into the oven for more challahs!

"Hurry up!" She called out to Rabbi Chanina's wife (thereby giving away her "secret" presence in the house as well), "Your challahs are ready and going to burn if you don't take them out right now!"

Rabbi Chanina's wife understood that G-d had granted them a miracle. She ran into the kitchen, and upon seeing her nosy neighbor she even took pains not to embarrass her. "I'm coming! I was just about to take the challahs out of the oven." The neighbor was ashamed of herself that she had attempted to denigrate this righteous woman. She hurriedly apologized and ran from the home.

Two-Strand Challah

These pretty challah shapes can be made large or small, but they look especially inviting when they are on the smaller side, which is why they are included in this chapter.

Roll out two equal-sized strands of dough, and lay them side by side.

Turn each one into an upside down "U" shape.

Lay one "U" over the center of the second "U."

At this point, the shape you have created should resemble a sort of "M" shape, and there are now four ends waiting to be braided.

Starting from the left side, take strand 2 and move it over and on top to the far right.

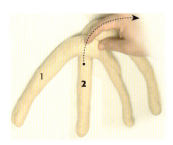

Then take (again, from the left side) strand 1 and move it to the middle.

Rotate now to the other direction and starting from the *right* side, take strand 2 and move it over and to the top of the far left.

Take what was strand 1 from the right side and move it to the middle.

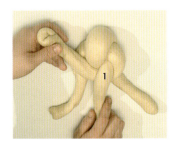

This should now take on the pattern of the Four-Braided Challah that we learned earlier, on page 50.

Continue braiding from one side to the other, until the dough is finished, then pinch together and tuck underneath to rise. These challahs will naturally have a larger, fatter end on the side you started from and will be thinner and smaller on the side where the braid ended.

Purim Breads · Hamantaschen Challah

Purim is a time of year that brings forth all sorts of creativity in many people. Presented here are three types of challah that can be done for the main meal on Purim day.

FOR ABOUT 45 MEDIUM SIZE (see picture on the right) HAMANTASHEN CHALLAHS:

Both recipes in these pictures were made using the regular white challah recipe.

FILLING:
- *5 large onions*
- *6 cloves garlic*
- *¼ cup olive oil*
- *Salt and pepper to taste*

These challahs come out in a small, triangular shape, and you can fill them with any filling of your choice. Because they are usually served at a meat meal, these were stuffed with a mixture of sautéed onions, garlic, olive oil, and some salt and pepper to taste. They look very festive and come out tasting extraordinary. My kids, on the other hand, think that onions in their challahs are absolutely revolting! So theirs were filled with — you guessed it — white and black chocolate chips!

To make the filling, chop the onions and garlic. In a frying pan on medium heat, sauté the onions and garlic in the olive oil until golden. Season to taste with salt and pepper. Cool.

To shape, simply pull off pieces of dough and shape them into medium-sized balls, about the size of an average palm.

Flatten each piece so that it becomes a flat, but not thin, round of dough in front of you. Spoon a tablespoon or two of the onion mixture (or whatever you want to fill it with — my kids prefer to fill them with chocolate chips!) into the dough's center.

Pinch two sides up and together, then the opposite sides, thereby forming a triangle.

Leave a nice-sized hole with the onions showing so that when it bakes, you will still see its triangular shape. Place on your lined baking tray with the seam side DOWN, so that when it rises it will not split open.

Let rise for a half hour, then brush the outside with an egg glaze. Bake as directed for small challah rolls, and cool on a wire rack. Freeze until the day of use.

To serve warm, simply defrost them and place them, covered, in a warm oven for 15–20 minutes before serving.

More Purim Ideas...

LAST YEAR, ON PURIM DAY, *I went out with my family to a good friend for the main meal, something I have not done in over a decade. The hostess, my friend Devorah, was expecting a large crowd of both families and yeshivah students from her husband's yeshivah. An atmosphere of happiness and joviality was in the air.*

All of the women present had made something for the meal so that no one person, the hostess included, would be overburdened by making too much food. And, no, I did not make the bread; I had offered instead to make the meat for the main course.

For the first course, she served fruit smoothies in small, plastic wine cups, along with salads that covered the tables and the cutest little colorful bread rolls I had ever seen. They were round, in a shape that was vaguely familiar to me, and were baked with a maraschino cherry in each one's center, along with colored sprinkles around each cherry to make them appear festive, bright, and, well — full of Purim spirit!

As we sat there thoroughly enjoying every bite of those sweet rolls, I couldn't help thinking to myself what a GREAT picture they would make. I also couldn't help thinking how good they were; something about their taste kept tugging at my memory...

I turned to the person who had baked them and openly complimented her on those rolls, asking her where she got the cute idea from. To my incredible surprise she told me, "Last year there was a four-page article in a popular magazine about challah and different ways to shape them. It came out right before Rosh HaShanah; did you see it? Anyhow, that article showed some really nice ways to shape small rolls, and this is that recipe, as well as the flower-shaped rolls that were shown. All I did was add some color by including the candied cherries and the sprinkles, to celebrate the Purim holiday spirit."

I almost choked on my bread. The author and baker of that article was none other than — ME!! The editor of the magazine did mention to me afterwards how popular the article was, but it never occurred to me to what extent. When I revealed to this person that it had been my own article, we all laughed uproariously at the irony of the whole situation. Now, at least, I knew why the challahs tasted so familiar all along!! So in honor of Malka Mankoff's creative idea, we hereby present you with the picture that I envisioned in my mind's eye at that Purim meal...

Wine-Bottle Challah

Another creative Purim challah idea is to make a roll large enough to hold the bottles of wine inside them.

Use the same technique as used above for napkin-ring challahs on page 76.

Simply roll out a very long, thick piece of dough. Make a large circle out of it, leaving a long tail at the end.

Weave that tail of dough under and over the circle three times, until you have a large ring of dough, with a large hole in the middle.

Or, alternatively, simply take two very long pieces of dough and then twist them over each other, making a twisted rope of dough. Then connect this into a circle shape.

Take an empty tin can and clean it inside and out.

Lightly grease the bottom outside of the can. Place this can inside the large dough ring, and set on a lined baking tray to rise for 20–30 minutes.

Bake the challah with the can still inside the dough. When the ring is finished baking, allow it to cool for 10 minutes on a wire rack. Carefully remove the ring from the can, using a sharp knife to loosen it if you have to. You should have a hole large enough to go over any average-sized wine or grape juice bottle. Freeze until the day of use.

Chapter 5

Health
Challah &
Breads

Half Whole Wheat Challah

FOR 10 MEDIUM-SIZED CHALLAHS:

- 9 cups stone-ground whole wheat flour
- 11 cups sifted white flour
- 6–7 cups warm water
- 1½ cups light brown sugar
- 3½ oz./100 gm. fresh yeast
- 1¼ cups canola oil
- 1½ T. salt
- 3 eggs for glazing

Start this recipe the same way that the regular white flour recipe was put together.

Place the oil, 2 cups of warm water, sugar, and salt into the mixing bowl. Add 5 cups of each kind of flour to this and stir a bit.

In another small bowl, put the yeast together with 2 T. of sugar and add 1½ cups of warm water.

Cover the small bowl and allow the mixture to start activating. When it is bubbling and foamy, add it to the mixing bowl and start to mix the dough.

Add in another 3 cups of flour, either kind, and another cup of water. Mix and then turn off the mixer and allow the dough to start to rise for 10 minutes.

Mix again and add all the rest of the ingredients slowly, one cup at a time, until you reach a smooth, non-sticky consistency of dough. *If the dough sticks too much to the sides of the bowl, add in a bit more oil.*

After the dough is thoroughly prepared, separate challah with a *brachah*. Then grease a large (it will rise a lot) bowl with a fine layer of oil. Turn out the dough into this bowl and turn it several times so that the dough will be greased lightly on all sides.

Cover the bowl with a large plastic garbage bag and allow it to rise for 1 hour before punching down and shaping.

Alternatively, place the unrisen dough in the large garbage bag, with all the air taken out and knotted on top of the bag, and place it in the refrigerator overnight to be shaped early the next morning.

This dough will shape and handle the same way the pure white one did and comes out delicious when it is baked. It is an especially tasty treat when cut into slices, toasted, and then served spread with a bit of butter and sprinkled with some cinnamon and sugar on top.

Pure Whole Wheat Challah

This recipe is from my proofreader, Yocheved Krems.

Place the yeast in the bottom of a large mixing bowl; crumble slightly with your hands.

Pour ¼ cup of the sugar on top. Add 2 cups warm water to cover it, then cover the bowl and let the yeast proof for 5–8 minutes. Add 13 cups of the flour, the oil, the rest of the sugar, and eggs. **Start to mix** while adding in another 3 cups of water. Add in the salt and continue to knead. It should resemble a thick batter at this point.

Turn off the mixer and cover the bowl again.

Let the mixture rest for 10 minutes. Turn the mixer back on and slowly add the remaining flour while mixing and adding in water at the same time until a smooth, slightly sticky dough is formed.

This can be done by hand as well as by mixer. Keep mixing until the dough is uniformly mixed. Add small amounts of water and oil as needed until the dough is soft and pliable, but neither too dry nor too wet

When done, separate challah with a *brachah*. Then transfer the dough to a very large, oiled bowl to rise, covered with plastic and a towel, for 45 minutes.

If the shaping will be done only much later on in the day or the next morning, grease your hands with oil, pat the dough all over and place it in a large garbage bag. Remove all air and seal it on top with a strong knot.

Place the dough in the refrigerator until ready for shaping.

Punch the dough down and then shape and bake as directed for regular white challahs.

Dijon Rye Bread

INGREDIENTS FOR TWO LOAVES:

- 4 tsp. dry yeast
- 2–3 T. brown sugar
- 1⅓ cup warm water
- 3 cups finely ground whole wheat flour (bread or pastry flour)
- 1 cup rye flour
- ⅔ cup Dijon mustard or spicy brown mustard
- 1 egg for glazing, or just the egg white

This recipe was graciously given to me by Chef Lambiase, director of the Jerusalem School of Kosher Culinary Arts. www.jskca.co.il

Place some of the yeast with some of the sugar and warm water into your mixing bowl.

Let stand for 10 minutes. Then add in the rest of the liquid and the yeast. Add the flours and make a well. Add the Dijon mustard.

Stir and knead well until it becomes a pliable dough. Cover and let the dough rest in a warm area until it doubles in size.

Punch down the dough and cut it in half.

Shape it into loaves and place each in a loaf pan that has been sprayed with oil or non-stick spray.

Make one slit down the length of the loaf, in its center, and let the dough rise in a warm area, covered loosely with plastic, for about 20 minutes or until the dough springs back, leaving no imprint when pressed.

Brush with the egg glaze and bake 35-40 minutes at 375°F/190°C until golden brown on top and bottom.

Tofu Bread Sticks

INGREDIENTS FOR 30–40 SMALL ROLLS OR OVER 70 BREADSTICKS

- 4 T. dry yeast
- ¾ cup light brown sugar
- 5 cups warm water
- 1½ cups canola oil
- 7 cups whole wheat flour
- 6 cups rye flour
- 1 cup wheat germ
- ½ cup ground sesame seeds
- ¼ cup bran
- 1½ T. salt
- 10.5 oz./300 gm. tofu, drained and shredded or crumbled
- 1 egg for glazing, or just the egg white

Place the dry yeast in the mixer bowl and add the sugar and 2 cups of the warm water to it. Cover the bowl and let it stand for five minutes.

Add in the oil, flours, and 2 more cups of warm water. Start to knead with the kneading hook of the mixer. Add in the wheat germ, ground sesame, bran, and salt. If the dough is tough or dry, add the rest of the water now. Knead until the mixture starts to resemble a smooth dough. Cover the dough lightly with a large plate or a piece of plastic and allow the dough to rest for about 10 minutes.

In the meantime, crumble or shred the tofu. Remove the cover from the dough and turn on the kneading hook again, on its lowest setting. Add in

the tofu bits and continue to knead until the tofu bits are incorporated well into the dough. If the dough is too stiff, add in drops of water and oil a little bit at a time until the dough is smooth and pliable. Turn off the mixer.

Separate challah without a *brachah*.

Grease a large bowl with a very fine layer of canola oil, or spray the bowl with cooking spray.

Turn the dough out into this greased bowl and knead by hand to incorporate all the pieces that may still be somewhat dry, or that were stuck to the sides and bottom of the mixing bowl. Do this for several minutes until the dough is uniform and pliable. The dough should be mildly sticky,

but still quite firm. Cover the top of the dough with a piece of plastic and then place the entire bowl in a large plastic garbage bag. Remove the air and tie it at the top. Leave it to rise until double in bulk, about 1 hour, or overnight in the refrigerator.

Preheat the oven to 400°F/200°C.

TO MAKE BREADSTICKS:

Cut off a section of the dough. Lightly flour your working surface and roll out the dough into a rectangle in front of you, to about a ½ inch / 1½ cm. thickness. If it is too thin, it will break when you attempt to pull it off the working surface. Make even strips about 2 inches / 5 cm. wide, and about 6 inches / 15 cm. down. If the strips are too long, simply slice them in half to create a more uniform length to your breadsticks. Place them on a lined baking tray about ¾ inch / 2 cm. apart from each other to allow them room when baking.

Let them rise for only 15 minutes. Gently brush them with the egg or egg white and bake for 15–20 minutes until golden light brown; if they do not look browned, check the bottom of the breadsticks. If they are browned on the bottom, they are done. These come out crispy on the outside and soft and moist on the inside.

TO MAKE ROLLS:

Spray two or three muffin trays with cooking spray. Roll the dough into small-sized balls (about 2½ inches in diameter). Cover the trays loosely with plastic, and allow them to rise for 45 minutes. Brush them with the egg and bake until they are light golden brown on top and bottom, about 20–25 minutes.

Because these sticks/rolls are filled with whole grains as well as the tofu for protein, they are almost a whole meal by themselves! Enjoy them with soup and salad for a delicious and nutritious repast anytime.

Mixed Wheat Loaves

The first time you make this recipe, it is worthwhile to try it with the half/half mixture, and to keep the 5-6 cups white flour in it. After you have tasted it and seen how the texture appeals to you, then you can decide how much white flour you want to replace with whole wheat.

When buying whole wheat flour, there are different kinds available, with different percentages of bran. Ask the clerk at your local health food store to really get a better understanding of what kind of whole wheat you would want to use. Some brands of whole wheat are also ground more finely than others; the finer it is ground, the lighter it is to look at and to work with.

Proof the fresh yeast with 1 T. of the sugar, and one cup of the warm water. Cover the bowl and allow it to start activating.

Place the oil, remaining sugar, salt, and 2 cups of warm water into the mixing bowl. Add the 8 cups of whole wheat flour. Add the activated yeast mixture. Mix all of this together until if forms a thick paste. Cover the bowl and let it rise for 10–15 minutes.

Uncover the bowl and add 2 more cups of flour. Start to mix with the dough hook and keep adding the rest of the flours and the water, one cup at a time, until you have a firm, moist, but not too sticky dough. Separate challah with a *brachah.*

Grease another large bowl (this rises a lot) and remove the dough from the mixer into this large bowl. Turn the dough over once in order to grease it on all sides. Cover the dough with a large piece of plastic, and then a large cloth on top of that. Allow to rise for 45 minutes to 1 hour. Check it occasionally to ensure that it does not rise so much that it spills out of the bowl onto the countertop!

Slice the dough into four equal sections. Remove one section and cut it in half. Roll out the piece of dough with your rolling pin and then roll up into a short, fat log. Continue doing this to each of the remaining pieces of dough in your bowl. Allow the logs to rise, covered, for 10 minutes.

Grease your hands lightly with oil and gently roll the logs, tapering the end, into a fat loaf shape. Place the dough in greased or lined loaf pans. Using a sharp knife, make a long slit down the center of each loaf, about one to two inches in depth. Allow to rise for 45 minutes, until double in size.

Preheat the oven to 350°F / 180°C while the dough is rising.

Mix the 2 egg whites and the 2 T. cold water together. Brush the loaves with this mixture.

To make the breads look more "whole grainy," you can now sprinkle them with any, or a combination, of the following: oats, sunflower seeds, caraway seeds, poppy seeds, or sesame seeds (brown sesame seeds make a special presentation).

Bake for 40 minutes, or until dark golden in color on both top and bottom.

This recipe is great fun to make and enjoy with the whole family on a cold winter's day, when all the kids are home because school is closed due to blizzard warnings. Serve with a hearty pot of fresh vegetable soup.

Rye and Flaxseed Buns

I created this recipe from scratch after overbuying on ground flax and ground whole sesame seeds. It is rich in dietary fiber, has the flax for Omega-3 fatty acids, and the whole sesame, which is a good source of calcium. All combined, this bread is tasty and nutritious, and became an instant hit with my family and guests.

In the mixer bowl, pour the yeast granules, ¼ cup of the light brown sugar, and 1 cup of the warm water. Cover the bowl and let it activate for 5 minutes.

Add the oil, soy milk, and 2 more cups of warm water. Add in the whole wheat flour, wheat germ, ground sesame seeds, and flax.

Start to knead this with your mixer until it turns into a thick mixture. Add the rest of the water and the rye flour in one cup increments, until you have a workable dough. If the dough is not pliable, add more drops of water and oil, alternating between the two, until you have a good dough that does not stick to the sides of your mixing bowl. Turn off the mixer. Separate challah without a *brachah*.

Grease a large bowl and turn out the dough into this bowl. Turn the dough over one more time so it is greased on all sides. Cover loosely with plastic wrap and then with towels and allow it to rise for an hour. It will grow at least twice its size.

Punch down. There are many ways that this dough can be shaped. To make this into simple hot–dog-shaped buns, simply roll out thick logs as usual, but allow them to rise directly on your lined baking trays. To make small muffin-shaped rolls, grease a muffin tin well with cooking spray and make medium sized "knots" out of the logs. Then allow them to rise inside the muffin holders. To make simple rolls, shape them into small rounds with your hands and let them rise directly on the baking trays.

Preheat the oven to 350°F / 180°C for 20 minutes prior to baking. Brush the rolls with the egg white. If desired, sprinkle sesame seeds on top of the rolls, or cornmeal.

Bake for 20 minutes, until the rolls are golden brown on top and bottom.

Tastes amazing straight out of the oven topped with butter and accompanied by a hearty salad!

Water Challah

This recipe is from my proofreader, Deena Nataf, who got it from her dear friend, Chassidah Levy, o.b.m.

Water challah is "true bread" (i.e., ha-motzi) according to all halachic opinions. A recipe such as this one is common among Jews of German and Sephardic descent.

INGREDIENTS:

- 9 - 9½ cups finely ground whole wheat or white flour
- 1½ T. dry yeast
- 1½ T. sugar
- ¾ cup + 1 T. (200 ml.) warm water
- 2-3 additional cups warm water
- ¾ cup + 2 T. oil
- 1 T. salt
- 1 egg for glazing
- sesame seeds and/or shelled sunflower seeds for sprinkling on the challahs

Put 8½ cups of flour in a bowl and make a well. Mix yeast, sugar and the 200 ml. of water together and pour it into the well. Cover and let stand for 10 minutes. The yeast should have begun activating. Mix somewhat and then add the oil and salt. Continue to mix while adding the additional 2-3 cups of water, in ½-cup increments, until you have a smooth, slightly sticky, but not dry dough. Don't be afraid to add lots of water, as the challah will come out very moist this way.

Knead the dough by hand for 10 minutes, adding small bits of flour from the remaining 1 cup as needed. Coat your hands with a very thin film of oil while kneading the dough; this will help to retain its elasticity as well as keep it from sticking to your hands.

Separate challah without a *brachah*. Cover and let rise 1½ hours. Punch it down well all over and knead for another 2-3 minutes, not more. Form into loaves or challahs and let them rise, covered loosely with plastic, for 45 min. – 1 hour, until double in size.

Start to preheat the oven at 400˚F / 200˚C approximately 20 minutes before you are going to bake the challahs. Beat 1 whole egg with a fork, and glaze the challahs. Sprinkle the tops

with either sesame seeds, sunflower seeds, or a combination of both.

Bake for 1 hour. Jews of German descent prefer their challah soft on the inside but very crusty on the outside, and this is why these challahs are baked so long. If you bake for less time, the bottoms of the challahs won't be as brown. The first time you make this recipe, check the challahs after 45 minutes. If they appear too dark on top to you, or you are afraid they will burn, cover them loosely with foil and continue to bake for the last 15 minutes. If you don't enjoy such a thick crust on your challahs, take them out after 45 minutes. Remove from pan to wire rack and cool completely. Then wrap in freezer bags and freeze until the day of use.

Spelt Bread or Challah

Spelt flour is a very nice alternative for those who are wheat sensitive. It is healthy and quite tasty, as well, so it can be enjoyed by just about anyone.

INGREDIENTS FOR 6 LARGE OR 8 MEDIUM-SIZED CHALLAHS:

- *65 grams fresh yeast*
- *a little more than 5 cups warm water*
- *1 ¼ cups light brown sugar*
- *17 cups spelt flour (this comes to just about 5 lbs. or 2¼ kilo of spelt flour)*
- *1 ½ T. salt*
- *1 cup oil*

Crumble the yeast into the mixing bowl. Add 2 cups of warm water and ¼ cup of sugar on top of it. Cover the bowl and let it start to activate for 5–10 minutes.

Add 10 cups of flour, the salt, and the oil. Mix and knead with the dough hook until it resembles a thick batter. Let it rest, covered, for 10 minutes.

Knead again while adding in all the rest of the flour. Add the water a bit at a time until you have a smooth and pliable, slightly sticky dough.

Separate challah with a *brachah*.

Turn the dough out into a large, well-oiled bowl. Cover the dough with a sheet of plastic and then a large towel and allow it to rise for 40 minutes. If you will not have time to shape and bake right away, place the dough, covered well with plastic, in the refrigerator for a few hours or overnight.

Spelt dough rises a bit differently than wheat dough. It is lighter, and therefore should not be left to rise as long as wheat dough.

Preheat the oven to 350°F / 180°C while you are shaping the loaves. Add a tray of water to the bottom rack of the oven to add moisture during the baking process, since you won't be using an egg glaze.

Punch down the dough and start to shape the loaves. When rolling out the strands, let them rest for only 1 minute before rolling out and braiding them. Shape and allow the dough to rise for 35 minutes. *Do not let the dough rise too much or the bread/challah will fall flat when it is baked.*

Spray the challahs with a thin film of clear water and sprinkle on seeds of your choice, if desired. Bake for 35–40 minutes, until dark golden brown on top. Place on a wire rack to cool. Freeze until use.

...There is something about bread, or rather, challah in particular, that is singularly unique. Whenever I want to give a special gift to someone, to say "thank you," or "welcome home," or simply "I care," I bake challahs for them. People appreciate it so immensely and it makes me feel so good to share ... because I've come to see that my challahs are also an extension of my heart.

Spelt flour can
also be purchased
as whole grain spelt
flour – which is darker,
or as white spelt flour
– which is lighter. The
challahs depicted here
are made from a half-
half mixture of both of
these spelt flours.

Spelt or White Flour French Bread

INGREDIENTS:

- 2½ cups warm water
- 2 packages active dry yeast or 4 tsp. instant dry yeast or 35 grams of fresh yeast granules
- 1 T. salt
- 1 T. oil
- 6–7 cups flour of your choice
- ¼ cup corn meal
- 1 egg white
- 1 T. cold water

This recipe works equally well with white flour, whole wheat flour, or spelt; or a mixture of any of them.

In an American-sized oven, this will make two long French breads; in a European-sized oven, it will make three slightly smaller ones.

Dissolve the yeast in the warm water.

Add salt, oil, and 6 cups of flour. Mix well. Keep adding the rest of the flour until you have a dough. It will be somewhat sticky. Separate challah without a *brachah* if you use 7 or more cups of flour.

Turn the dough into a large, greased bowl and then turn it over again so that the dough will be lightly greased on all sides. Cover with plastic wrap and let the dough rise until double in size, about 1 hour.

Punch the dough down. Divide it in half and roll each piece into an approximately 12x15-inch rectangle. Roll up this rectangle from the long side, tapering the ends a bit and sealing it as you

roll. If you're making three smaller ones, divide the dough into thirds and roll each piece into a rectangle of 10 x 12 inches.

Line a wide baking tray with parchment baking paper and sprinkle the paper with the corn meal.

Lay the French bread rolls onto the corn meal and with a sharp knife, make four diagonal cuts on the top of each roll, somewhat deep but not all the way through the roll.

Allow the shaped dough to rise for about an hour, until doubled in size.

Note: If you are using spelt flour, let the shaped dough rise for only 40 minutes, as spelt rises differently and the breads will have a slightly flatter appearance if

they rise for too long. Then bake as directed below.

Preheat the oven to 450°F/220°C. Place in the oven and bake for 25 minutes.

Mix together the egg white and one tablespoon of water; brush the bread with this mixture. Replace in the oven and bake for five more minutes.

The picture featured on the right is from whole grain spelt flour.

Rye Bread

INGREDIENTS FOR 25 SMALL ROLLS:

- 3 cups rye flour
- 3 cups white or spelt flour
- 1 T. salt
- 1 T. sugar or fructose
- ¾ cup warm water
- 2 tsp. dry yeast
- 1 cup soy milk
- 2 T. honey
- 1 T. canola oil
- 3 T. caraway seeds, optional
- ¼ cup cornmeal
- 1 egg white
- 2 T. cold water

Combine both flours and the salt. Stir a bit.

Take 4½ cups of this flour mixture and add to it the water, yeast, soy milk, sugar, honey, and oil. Mix for 2 minutes. Add the rest of the flour, a half a cup at a time, and keep mixing.

When everything is mixed in, knead a bit more. If it is too dry, add a bit more water. Knead for 10 minutes by hand or in the mixer.

If you are using caraway seeds, add them to the dough now.

Turn the dough into a large, greased bowl and then turn it over again so that the dough will be lightly greased on all sides. Then cover it with plastic wrap and let it rise for an hour or until double in size.

Punch the dough down and divide it in half.

Roll each half into a ball-like shape; let this rest for 10 minutes. Keep the dough covered with plastic wrap so it will not dry out.

TO MAKE LOAVES:
Simply flatten each piece of dough slightly with lightly greased hands and gently roll it back and forth until you have an oval-shaped loaf. Keep the ends a bit tapered.

Line a baking tray or loaf pan with baking paper and sprinkle the bottom with cornmeal.

Mix the egg white and water. Brush on the egg glaze *before* this bread starts to rise. Let the loaves rise uncovered for an hour.

Preheat the oven to 400°F/200°C and bake the loaves for 25 minutes or until done.

Here you see small "muffin" rolls made from this dough. These are excellent for the third meal on Shabbos, or for a party or brunch.

TO MAKE SMALL ROLLS:
(as featured here)
Roll out pieces of dough to be made into single strands. Then just tie each piece in a simple knot form.

Spray a muffin pan with cooking oil inside each muffin cup, as well as all over the top of the tray. This is to prevent the breads from sticking to the top of the muffin tray when they rise.

Place each knot inside a muffin cup. Allow to rise and then bake as directed.

Sourdough Bread

This recipe was graciously donated by David Sasson of Sasson's Gourmet Cuisine, Manchester.

MAKES ABOUT 6–8 AVERAGE-SIZED LOAVES.

This bread is made without any of the commercial bought yeast that is normally used in all breads. In order for the bread to rise, a culture has to be created first that will act in place of the yeast.

YEAST CULTURE:

- *1 cup plus 2 T. rye flour*
- *scant ⅔ cup apple juice*

  or scant ⅔ cup water + 1 tsp. vinegar
- *½ tsp. salt*

Mix this together by hand and leave it in a small plastic bowl. Sprinkle just a little more salt on top of the mixture and tightly cover the bowl with plastic wrap. Leave it to ferment in a warm place for at least five days.

After the five days, add this culture together with the following, in a larger bowl:

- *6⅓ cups (1½ liters) lukewarm water*
- *2 T. salt*
- *1 cup plus 2 T. rye flour*
- *5¼ cups wheat flour*
- *3 cups rye (or any whole grain) kernels**

* For those who don't have access to whole grain kernels, or don't want to add them in, the same amount of additional wheat flour may be substituted in its place.

This mixture should now resemble a thick cake batter. Leave it to sit again, covered as before, for another 24 hours. After the 24 hours, add into the mixture:

- *8 cups rye flour*
- *2 cups (½ liter) lukewarm water*
- *½ cup brown sugar*

Mix this all together. It should form a sticky dough. If the dough is too runny, add bits of wheat flour to it until you have a workable dough. Separate challah with a *brachah*. It's a good idea to also take a large fistful of this dough and put it aside, covered, in the refrigerator, so that it can be used as the culture for the next week's bread.

This bread is not easily shaped into braids, because of its stickiness. Make a standard loaf out of the dough and use loaf pans for this recipe so that the dough will rise up, rather than spread. The side of the loaf pans helps the bread to hold its shape best.

Fill the pans only halfway and leave them to rise for a few hours, until doubled in size. The rising time is much longer because you are relying on the natural yeast in the sourdough rather than commercial yeast. Preheat the oven to 350°F/180°C.

Whisk oil and water together in a small bowl and brush over the breads, so that they won't crack when they are baking. Bake at the bottom of the oven for 2 hours, but cover them loosely with foil after 1 hour so that the tops of the breads will not burn during the baking process.

Gluten-Free Bread

This recipe makes enough for one loaf in a bread machine. It can be made by hand as well.

- *2 cups brown rice flour*
- *1 cup potato starch*
- *¼ cup sugar*
- *2 tsp. xanthan gum**
- *1 tsp. salt*
- *¼ cup oil*
- *1¾ cup water*
- *1 tsp. vinegar*
- *1 egg*
- *2 egg whites*
- *1 tsp. unflavored gelatin, optional*
- *1 T. dry yeast*

* Xanthan gum is available in the United States at most local health food stores.

TO MAKE IN THE BREAD MACHINE:

Follow the instructions on your bread machine for which ingredients to put in first. Some machines say to put in the dry ingredients first; others say to put the wet ingredients first. Sprinkle the yeast on top of the mixture as the very last step.

TO MAKE BY HAND:

First, put the yeast in the warm water with 1 T. of the sugar and let it bubble. In the mixer bowl, add all other ingredients. Add the yeast mixture and knead until everything is fully mixed together. Place in a lined loaf pan. Allow to rise until double in size. Bake at 350°F/180°C until light brown and firm on top and bottom.

Delicious and filling, this recipe is a very big hit for those who cannot eat gluten — and even for those who can!

Oatmeal Raisin Rolls

**FOR 25 ROLLS
OR 2-3 LOAVES**

- 2 oz./50 gm. fresh yeast
- ½ cup warm water
- 1 T. light brown sugar
- 1 cup oatmeal (preferably not instant)
- ½ cup untoasted wheat germ
- ¼ cup ground flaxseed
- 1 T. salt
- 5 to 7½ cups sifted white flour *
- 3 eggs
- ½ cup canola oil
- ½ cup honey
- ½ cup light brown sugar
- 1½ cups warm water
- ½ cup dark raisins
- ½ cup white raisins
- 1-2 eggs for glazing
- sesame seeds for sprinkling on the breads

My mother gave me this recipe after she ate it at the home of a family friend. It's filled with taste and good-for-you grains …

Dissolve the yeast in ½ cup warm water and 1 T. sugar. Let this bubble up.

In a separate bowl, mix the dry ingredients: the oatmeal, wheat germ, ground flax, salt, and 5 cups of flour. Set aside.

In the mixer bowl, combine the eggs, oil, honey and sugar and beat well. Then add the yeast mixture. Add the rest of the warm water. Start adding

* Finely ground whole wheat pastry flour can be substituted here.

in the dry ingredients, about 2 cups at a time and start to knead in the mixer. While you are adding in the dry ingredients, add in the raisins also. Knead well until not sticky. Now is where the extra 2 ½ cups of flour comes in. Keep adding flour in, small bits at a time, until the dough is more uniform and workable. It will remain sticky; this is fine. Turn off the mixer.

Grease another bowl and turn the dough out into this bowl. Turn it over once so all sides of the dough are covered with a light coating of oil. Cover the bowl with plastic wrap and then a towel and leave

it to rise in a warm area for at least 2 hours, until double in size.

Punch down the dough and shape into rolls. Cover the rolls with plastic again and let them rise for about 1 hour.

Twenty minutes before the end of the rising time, preheat the oven to 350°F / 180°C.

Brush the oatmeal bread rolls with the egg glaze and sprinkle with sesame seeds. Bake until the top of the rolls are light golden brown and the bottom of the rolls are firm and golden as well.

Optional idea: to give it a different flavor, try adding 1 T. of ground cinnamon to the dry ingredients.

Chapter 6

Specialty Breads

Za'atar Challah

Za'atar is a blend of hyssop and several different spices. It is most often associated with Middle Eastern-style foods.

Prepare the challah dough as directed and shape individual small challahs as desired.

Lay the challahs out on baking trays lined with parchment baking paper and let rise until double in size.

Preheat oven. Brush challahs with egg glaze. Just before placing them in the preheated oven, brush them with a small amount of olive oil, and then sprinkle za'atar over each challah.

Bake as usual. *The aroma wafting from your kitchen will be truly exotic and the taste will definitely surprise you with its unique richness and flavor.*

These breads are often served together with more olive oil and za'atar available on the table for dipping the bread into as it is eaten.

Elisheva's Story

ABOUT THREE YEARS AGO *I had first heard about the power of doing the mitzvah of separating challah properly for the merit of oneself or even of someone else. I had mentioned the concept to my sister-in-law, Miriam, and she was very interested in organizing a group of 40 women to be "mafrish challah" with a brachah for the merit of her friend, Sarah.*

Sarah lived in the same community and was already married for seven years, but sadly, was still childless. Miriam wanted to give the merit of the mitzvah of separating challah to Sarah, as segulah to have children.

Miriam planned the challah baking with the other 40 or so women for the Shabbos after Pesach. About three months later, Miriam, who for health reasons was not supposed to have any more children, and who had organized the hafrashas challah for Sarah, discovered that she herself was expecting! Being a very sensitive person, Miriam started to worry about Sarah, and how Sarah might feel to see Miriam suddenly in maternity clothes.

But how could she hide her pregnancy? Miriam decided to call Sarah's sister, Leah, and thereby find out the best way to break the news to her. Leah started laughing. Sarah was also expecting!!! And Baruch Hashem they both had healthy children within just a few weeks of each other!

Garlic Bread

Using the Always Perfect No-Egg Challah recipe on page 32, simply roll out a medium-sized piece of dough.

Preheat the oven to 350°F / 180°C.

Squeeze several cloves of fresh garlic with a garlic press and spread this over the top of each piece of dough. Push the crushed garlic down into the dough slightly with your fingertips. Brush each piece of dough with olive oil.

Let the garlic breads rise for 15 minutes.

Bake for 15-20 minutes until the garlic bread is golden brown on top and bottom. This can be frozen for later use or served immediately, piping hot.

Another way to create delicious garlic bread is to slice open French bread and place it on a baking tray. Using olive oil or olive oil cooking spray, coat each piece. Sprinkle each piece with granulated garlic or, if you prefer, fresh crushed garlic. Toast for several minutes in a hot oven and serve immediately.

GARLIC BREADSTICKS

This is another variation for genuine garlic bread.

Preheat the oven to 375°F / 180°C.

Pull off small golf-sized pieces of dough and roll them out pencil-thin. Ten-inch lengths are very nice to work with, but any length you prefer is fine.

Lay the breadsticks on a lined baking tray and brush them lightly with olive or canola oil. Sprinkle them with granulated garlic. Bake immediately, without letting them rise, for 10-15 minutes until golden and crispy on the outside.

Pecan Challah

INGREDIENTS:
- *challah dough*
- *⅓ cup canola oil*
- *1 cup brown sugar*
- *1 ½ cups chopped pecans*
- *1 T. cinnamon*
- *egg glaze*

To chop the pecans, do not use the food processor. The pecans merely get stuck in the blades and cause the processor to overheat. Simply place them in a strong plastic bag, take a rolling pin, and start to roll and crush them on the work surface in front of you. For added measure,

you can always use your rolling pin to smack them a bit as well!

In a large bowl, mix together by hand the oil, brown sugar, chopped pecans, and cinnamon. Set aside.

To make a three-or four-braided pecan challah, when rolling out the dough pieces in order to make the strands, sprinkle a generous amount of pecan mix onto the dough before rolling it up into a log.

Allow the strands to rise for 5 minutes.

Then gently roll them out a bit more with your greased hands into longer, but not too thin, strands. Braid, rise, baste with the egg glaze, and bake it as you would regular challah. When you go to slice it open, there will be a delicious surprise inside each person's slice! Makes an excellent holiday or special-occasion treat.

Bagels

Mix 1½ cups flour, sugar, and salt in a mixing bowl. Set aside.

In another small bowl, place yeast, warm water, and 1T. sugar. Leave for a few minutes until it starts to activate.

Add this mixture to the mixture in the first bowl. Mix well. Add the rest of the flour and knead until a smooth and workable dough is formed.

Cover loosely and let rise for 20 minutes. Punch down and you can start to work.

Divide the dough into four sections.

Each section makes 4-5 balls of dough.

Roll each ball into a log and then pinch closed into a circle shape.

A great way to "pinch" this closed is to place your hand through the hole, then, with your hand still inside it, press down on the seam where the dough ends meet. It will help to seal it nicely and hold its shape better than just by being pinched together.

Leave to rise for 20 min. on parchment baking paper.

Place 5–6 inches of water into a large pot. Bring the water to a boil and drop the risen bagels inside.

Boil for 90 seconds exactly, (using a timer to keep track of the seconds). Then flip each one, and let them boil for another 90 seconds on their second side.

Remove immediately from the water with your tongs; place on a towel to drain slightly and cool.

Dip into toppings of your choice, such as sesame seeds, dried onions, granulated garlic, poppy seeds, coarse salt, or a mix of all.

Place the bagels on a baking tray lined with baking paper.

They may be placed close together as they will not rise any more. Bake for 20 minutes or until lightly browned all over at 325°F / 175°C. Cool on wire rack.

Whole Wheat Raisin Bagels

Mix 1 cup white flour, 2 cups whole wheat flour, cinnamon, and salt in a mixing bowl. Set aside.

In another small bowl, place yeast, warm water, and the brown sugar. Leave for a few minutes until it starts to activate.

Combine both mixtures and mix well. Toss the raisins in a small bowl separately with about ¼ cup of any flour; reserve them for later use.

Then add the rest of the ingredients to the flour/yeast mixture and knead until a smooth and workable dough is formed.

Cover loosely and let rise for 20 minutes. Punch down and you can start to work.

Make the logs for the bagels the same way as in the previous bagel recipe, except here you take the raisins you reserved from before and add them to the logs while shaping them.

Boil and bake these whole wheat bagels exactly the same way as in the previous bagel recipe.

If you would like them to have a brown sugar-cinnamon topping, simply dip each one into a mix of brown sugar and cinnamon right after they have been boiled, prior to baking them.

These are delicious served warm or toasted, smeared with cream cheese or any spread of choice.

Zucchini Bread

INGREDIENTS:

- ½ cup soy milk or water
- 1 tsp. salt
- 50 grams fresh yeast granules or 2 T. dry yeast
- ⅓ cup canola oil
- 2 cups spelt flour
- 2–2½ cups whole wheat flour
- ½ tsp. cinnamon
- 1 large zucchini or 2 small ones, unpeeled, scrubbed, and shredded
- 1 small onion, very finely diced
- ⅓ cup finely chopped walnuts or almonds

This recipe will make 2 loaf-size pans of bread, or you can cut off pieces of dough and roll them into small rolls or pinwheels.

Slightly warm the soy milk, mix in the salt, and pour into the bowl of your mixer. Sprinkle on the yeast granules. Add in the oil and both flours, reserving the last ½ cup of whole wheat flour for later.

Start to knead with the dough hook of the mixer.

Add the zucchini and onion to the mixing dough. Knead another 3 minutes and add in the cinnamon and finely chopped nuts. Continue to knead until the dough is soft but not too sticky.

Add in just enough of the extra flour to keep the dough from being sticky; knead it until the dough is soft and workable. If the dough is too dry, add in small amounts of water or soy milk, a teaspoon at a time, until it is a nice consistency.

Grease your hands with a very fine layer of oil and coat the ball of dough on all sides with your greased hands.

Lay it back into the mixing bowl, cover the bowl with a damp cloth, and allow it to rest in a warm place for 45 minutes, or until it has doubled in size.

Now punch down the dough and divide it in half.

Bake at 350°F / 180°C until the breads are deep golden brown on top and bottom.

Soft Pretzels

Blessing: mezonos

FOR 24 MEDIUM-SIZED PRETZELS:

- 40 grams fresh yeast or 1½ oz. fresh yeast granules
- 2 cups warm water
- ½ cup sugar
- 2 tsp. salt
- ¼ cup soft margarine or vegetable shortening
- 1 egg
- 6½–7½ cups flour
- 1 additional egg yolk + 2 T. water
- coarse salt or sesame seeds

Dissolve the yeast in the warm water. Pour this into a bowl and add the sugar, salt, margarine, egg, and 3 cups of flour. Mix until smooth.

Keep adding flour and mixing until the dough is a smooth and somewhat stiff consistency. Separate challah without a *brachah*. Cover the bowl well and leave in the refrigerator to rise for 2 hours.

Divide the dough into four sections. Each section should make 6 smaller portions of dough.

Roll out each small portion into long, thin strands and shape into pretzel shapes.

Leave them to rise, covered loosely with plastic, until double in size, about 25 minutes.

Mix the egg yolk and 2 T. water together. Brush this glaze over each pretzel with a soft-bristled pastry brush. Sprinkle pretzels with coarse salt or sesame seeds and bake at 400°F/200°C for 15 minutes, until golden brown and crispy on top.

These pretzels are a fun and special treat and can be frozen after they are baked.

Additional ideas:

For cheese pretzels, roll out each portion of dough with a rolling pin. Sprinkle with grated Parmesan or mozzarella cheese and roll up into a log. Gently roll out this log until it is as long and thin a strand as possible. Continue as directed above by twisting these rolls into pretzel shapes and bake as directed.

For whole wheat pretzels, substitute light brown sugar for the white sugar and use 4 cups whole wheat flour plus 2½–3½ cups white. Continue with the rest of the recipe as directed above.

Onion Bagel Strips

This recipe was donated by Bentzion Goldstein of Ramat Beit Shemesh, Israel.

MAKES FOUR MEDIUM "STRIPS" OR SIX SMALL ONES.

- 2½ tsp. dry yeast
- 1 cup warm water
- 2 tsp. sugar
- 1 tsp. salt plus another ½ tsp. for sprinkling later on
- 2½ cups flour
- ½ cup matzo meal or an additional ½ cup flour
- ¼ cup olive oil
- 1 large onion, diced
- 2 tsp. paprika
- 2 tsp. granulated garlic

In the mixing bowl, dissolve the yeast in the warm water. Add the sugar. Add 2 cups of flour and 1 tsp. salt and start to mix it together. Pour in bits of the matzo meal and small amounts of the rest of the ½ cup of flour until the dough is stiff, but not hard.

Place the dough on a lightly floured board or counter and knead for five minutes. Grease a large plastic bowl and turn the dough into the bowl, then turn it over once so that all sides of the dough will be lightly greased.

Cover the dough with plastic and allow it to rise until double in size, about 1 hour.

Punch down the dough several times and let it rest for five minutes.

Preheat the oven to 350°F / 180°C.

In the meantime, dice the onion and take out the olive oil. Cut the dough into four or six even pieces and roll them out to resemble fat logs. Brush the tops of these logs with the olive oil. Sprinkle each generously with the diced onion and press the onions down gently into the dough with your fingertips. Sprinkle the tops of the logs with the rest of the salt, paprika, and garlic.

Bake until the bagel strips are light golden brown and crispy on top and bottom, about 20-30 minutes. Serve straight out of the oven.

TIP:
You can add guacamole seasoning mix to the tops of your bagel strips as well for a really interesting and different flavor.

Chapter 7

Middle Eastern Breads

AND ACCOMPANIMENTS

Saluf

The following four recipes are all from Malkie Sharabi

Saluf, as the Yemenites and Sephardim call this bread, is a Yemenite tradition at every Shabbos meal instead of the traditional braided challah loaves most of us are used to seeing. They resemble flat pitas but are baked a special way rendering them roasted on top and with a distinctively different flavor and aroma than ordinary store-bought pitas.

They are traditionally served with two side dishes, Chilbah and Resek. Chilbah is the green dip as seen in the pictures here, and there are many traditions of its various health remedies. Resek is simply a sauce. It is made from fresh tomatoes, onions, garlic, and spices pureed together and cooked over a low flame for 2–3 hours. A typical Yemenite table features saluf in abundance, and several dishes each of chilbah and resek for everyone to dip right in and enjoy. Delicious and exotic.

INGREDIENTS:

- 50 gm. fresh yeast or 2½ T. instant dry yeast
- 5–6 cups warm water
- 1½ T. sugar
- 2 T. + 1 tsp. salt
- 2 T. oil
- 7 cups (1 kilo) whole wheat flour
- 6 cups white flour

If using fresh yeast, bubble it in one cup water and 1 T. sugar. Wait for it to activate and rise a bit.

In a mixing bowl, add sugar, salt, oil, and 2 cups each of water and whole wheat flour. Sprinkle on the yeast, if you are using dry. If you used fresh yeast, add the yeast/water mixture now. Mix well. Keep adding flour and the rest of the water until a smooth, doughy mixture is formed. It will be somewhat sticky at first. Separate challah with a *brachah*.

Cover the bowl and let it rise for 10–15 minutes. Knead again briefly and let it rise, covered, for 1 hour until it is double in size.

Sprinkle your working surface with more flour.

Pull off handfuls of dough and roll them into individual balls. Roll each ball on the floured surface so it will be coated with a fine layer of flour. Leave these to rest for 10 minutes on a lightly floured surface.

Stretch each ball of dough between your fingers gently in order to get a wider circle of dough, but do not stretch it too thin. Heat up the saluf pan;

Immediately place it in the saluf pan and begin to

broil them one at a time. If you do not have a saluf pan, you can also broil these in your oven. However, they do come out much more authentic when they are done with the actual saluf pan, as seen in the photo on your right.

To bake the saluf in your oven, turn on your top element to 375°F / 190°C and wait until it turns red hot. Spray a baking tray with cooking spray and place the saluf on it. Broil one side until it is a nice roasted color. This will probably take less than 8 minutes. Watch it so that it does not burn. Flip them over and do the second side. Remove them promptly from the oven when done.

As each saluf is completed, leave it on a wire rack to cool off, and keep broiling the rest of the balls until they are all done. After they are cool, wrap them well in heavy plastic bags and freeze until they are needed. If they are to be used on the same day, simply wrap them when cool and leave them on the table, wrapped, until the meal begins. If they are left out too long, they tend to dry out.

Chilbah and Schug

In order to make real chilbah, you must have what is known as schug. If you can buy schug in the store, chilbah is that much easier to make. If not, here is a recipe for genuine schug, but please be careful; the ingredients are very, very spicy and sometimes can burn the skin on one's hands. It is therefore advisable, especially when making this recipe the first time, to use latex gloves.

GREEN SCHUG*

- ¼ cup water
- 2 whole HEADS (not individual cloves) of garlic, peeled
- 2 large bunches of kusbarah; this is known in English as coriander or Chinese parsley. (In Israel, this is equivalent to two whole packages of the bug-free variety.)
- 5 green hot peppers, washed and seeded
- 1 dark green regular pepper, washed and seeded
- 1 T. salt
- 2 tsp. cumin
- 2 T. black pepper

* You can substitute red peppers for the green (hot and regular) and make red schug.

Place water and then all other ingredients into a blender/food processor and puree. Refrigerate until use.

This is not a regular pepper, it's the short, thin version that has a very hot spicy flavor when cooked or pickled.

NOW, BACK TO MAKING CHILBAH:

Chilbah is known in English as fenugreek. It can be bought as grains or already ground. If bought as grains, it must be ground first before use.

- *1 cup chilbah powder*
- *1 T. salt*

Place these in a large bowl and cover it with water to soak. Cover the bowl, place in the refrigerator, and soak overnight.

To remove some of the "heat" from the pepper, cur away the inner white membrane at the same time that you remove the seeds.

The next day, pour out the water. Beat the remaining "mush" with the wire whisk in a mixer on high speed for 3 minutes. Turn down the speed and, while it is still mixing, add:

- *1 T. salt*
- *1 ½ cups water (Add this slowly and slow down the beater so it won't splash all over.)*
- *½ cup schug (If you like the chilbah spicier and hotter, just add more schug!)*

Beat until well blended, about another 3 minutes. This makes a lot at once, but it can be used immediately or frozen in small containers until needed.

Tomato Dip – "Resek"

Clean the onion and garlic and place in a food processor that has been fitted with the sharp "S" blade. Clean, but do not peel, the tomatoes and remove the stem and core from each one; cut in halves or fourths and add to the food processor. Add in salt, ¼ tsp. pepper, and olive oil. Puree until smooth; it will retain some chunkiness, but that is how it is supposed to look.

Transfer to a pot that has a good lid and cook until the boiling point. Turn down the flame, remove the lid so that the steam can escape, and continue to simmer for about 2 hours, until it thickens. The smell this creates as it is simmering is absolutely delicious. Cool slightly and refrigerate until ready to serve. Serve in small bowls around the table.

Another variation of this dish is called "matbucha." This is a very spicy, Middle Eastern food, which is made the same way, only adding more black pepper (another ½ tsp.), and one small green hot pepper.

Add this in along with all the tomatoes when pureeing the vegetables. When it cooks, it will also smell wonderful, but it will have a mighty powerful kick to it!

Kubana

Make a recipe of saluf. Knead the dough by hand for several minutes before beginning.

Pull off small pieces of dough and roll them into balls as mentioned in the saluf recipe.

This time, put a heaping amount of flour into a bowl and dredge each ball of dough in this flour.

There are now two ways to prepare the kubana dough. There is a special "kubana pot" designed for making this special bread. However, it can also be made in any good pot that has a cover and is oven-proof.

To bake this in the oven, coat the bottom of the pot with a layer of oil, not too fine, not too thick — about one inch deep. Place the balls of

dough that have been dredged in flour into the pot in a circle, with one ball in the center. It will resemble a flower.

Cover the pot with its lid and allow it to rise for 30 minutes. While it is rising, preheat the oven to 350°F/180°C. Bake, covered, for 45–50 minutes, until golden brown on all sides.

Uncover and bake for another 10–15 minutes until the top is browned as well. Flip it out of the pot and let it cool on a wire rack. Wrap well in plastic and freeze until use.

To bake this on the stovetop, arrange the dough balls the same way in the oiled pot. Allow it to rise for 30 minutes. Cover tightly with its lid and allow it to simmer on a small flame, covered the whole time, for 45–50 minutes.

This is how the kubana will look after being on the stovetop in a regular pot for 45 minutes. Then flip it out of the pot and place it, right-side/flower-side up, on a baking tray and bake for another 15 minutes, same temperature as mentioned above, until golden brown on top.

No-Pocket Pitas

INGREDIENTS FOR 12 MEDIUM-SIZED PITAS:

- 35–40 gm. fresh yeast or 1½ oz. dry yeast
- 3–3½ cups warm water
- 2 tsp. sugar
- 8–9 cups flour
- 1 T. salt

In a small bowl, place the yeast, ½ cup water, and the sugar. Cover the bowl and allow the yeast to activate and bubble.

In a large bowl, put the flour and the salt. Stir together a bit. Make a well in the middle of this flour mixture and add the activated yeast, plus another 2½ cups of warm water. Stir together with a fork until it starts to form a dough.

Then, using your hands, knead until the mixture becomes soft but not too sticky. If it is not soft, add a bit more water. If it is too watery, add a bit more flour. Separate challah without a *brachah*. Cover the dough and allow it to rise for 1 hour or until double in size.

Pinch off pieces of dough until there are 12 equal-sized balls. Roll each ball in a bit more flour,

and spread or roll each one out until it is at least twice its original diameter.

Heat a wide, heavy-duty frying pan on a small flame until hot, about 4–5 minutes.

Leave the pan ungreased! There is no oil used when "frying" pitas on the stovetop!

When the pan is hot, quickly place your pita on it and try to spread it out again as much as possible.

This picture features a smaller-sized pita.

Cover the frying pan and let the pita cook on a low flame for about 5 minutes. It should be somewhat browned on that side. Then flip it over and allow it to cook, again covered, for another 5 minutes. The first one or two times you do this, check to insure the pita is not burning.

Remove immediately from the pan and place it on a dry towel. Wrap it up and continue with the next pita until all the dough is finished.

Keep the pitas wrapped in the towel and place them in a plastic bag until use, to prevent drying out. Best served fresh, but can also be frozen for later use.

Baked Pitas

Another version of pitas can be made from the same dough. Although these pitas start off the same, the difference in how they are handled and baked makes for a completely different texture and taste.

Prepare Dough as for No-Pocket Pitas on page 154.

After the dough has risen, preheat your oven to 350°F / 180°C.

Separate the dough into 12 pieces as in the previous recipe, and roll each piece in a bit of flour.

With your hands, flatten each piece into a circle, not too thick and not too thin. Prick it with a fork in several places.

Line a baking tray with parchment baking paper and grease lightly with a cooking spray or with a very fine layer of oil. Place the pitas on the tray with at least 1 inch of space between them and slide into the oven to bake for 30–40 minutes, until browned on top. Wrap each pita in a towel and when cooled, place the wrapped pitas into a plastic bag until serving. These come out crispy on the outside and soft and light on the inside. Delicious!

More Pita Ideas

Here are two more ideas that can be done with any store-bought or homemade pocket pitas.

SESAME "CRACKERS"

- *several pitas*
- *olive oil or cooking spray*
- *sesame seeds*
- *za'atar spice*

Slit open several pitas. With a pastry brush, brush each one with olive oil, or just spray them with olive oil cooking spray.

Sprinkle on sesame seeds. If you want some of the "crackers" to be za'atar-flavored, sprinkle on some za'atar as well.

Cut each one into eight triangles, pizza-style. Place on a lined baking tray and toast in your oven at 325°F/170°C for about 10 minutes, until it is golden and crispy. Serve immediately with whatever dips you choose.

ROASTED PITAS

- *several pocket pitas, slit open. Prepare one per person, plus an additional two for extras*
- *olive oil or canola oil*
- *large frying pan*
- *za'atar*
- *granulated garlic, optional*

Here's another idea for using za'atar pitas. Shortly before serving, heat a large skillet and maintain its heat on a medium-to-small flame. Mix some olive oil and za'atar (and garlic if you wish) in a small bowl and brush each pita with this mixture. Lay it, oiled side down, on the hot skillet and "fry" it a bit on both sides. Serve immediately as a tasty appetizer or with a choice of dips and salads on the side.

Chapter 8

Fun & Different Ideas

Cinnabon Cinnamon Rolls

Blessing: "mezonos"

MAKES 12–20 ROLLS

DOUGH:

- 2¼ tsp. dry yeast
- 1 cup warm milk
  (use soy or rice milk if making it non-dairy)
- ½ cup sugar
- ⅓ cup butter or margarine, melted
- 1 teaspoon salt
- 2 eggs
- 4 cups white flour

FILLING:

- 1 cup packed brown sugar
- 2½ T. cinnamon
- ⅓ cup margarine, softened

ICING:

- ½ cup butter or margarine, softened
- 1 ½ cups powdered sugar
- ¼ cup (2 oz.) cream cheese
  (if making non-dairy, use tofu cream cheese)
- ½ tsp. vanilla extract

To make the dough, dissolve the yeast in warm milk in a large bowl. Mix together the sugar, butter or margarine, salt, and eggs. Add the flour and mix well.

Knead this dough into a large ball. Place in a lightly greased bowl, cover it, and let it rise for 1 hour.

Punch down the dough and roll it out on a lightly floured surface.

Cut 2–3- inch-long strips from the dough. Combine the filling ingredients in a bowl.

Spread margarine over the dough and sprinkle some of the filling on each strip.

Roll up each strip as a pinwheel and lay on a lined baking tray to rise.

Preheat oven to 400°F / 200°C.

Let the rolls rise again until double in size, about 30 minutes. Bake 10 to 15 minutes, or until light brown on top.

Combine icing ingredients while the rolls are baking. Beat well with an electric mixer until the icing is fluffy.

Coat each bun generously with icing — while hot! Freezes well.

Enjoy!

Rebbetzin Meisels' Onion Croissants

These are best served warm, and they make a great addition to a bowl of hot soup!

MAKES 16 LARGE OR 32 SMALL CROISSANTS

- 1 oz. / 25 gm. yeast
- ½ cup sugar
- 1¼ cups warm water
- 3 cups flour
- 3 cups high gluten flour
- 2 eggs
- ½ cup oil
- ¾ T. salt

FILLING:

- 2 large onions, diced
- ¼ cup canola or olive oil
- ½ cup breadcrumbs
- ½ tsp. salt
- ¼ tsp. black pepper

Blessing: "ha-motzi"

Place the yeast, some of the sugar, and half the warm water in a small bowl. Let the yeast start to bubble and activate.

In the mixing bowl, add everything else. Add in the yeast mixture and knead together until it forms a smooth and pliable dough. Cover the dough in a large garbage bag and allow it to rise until double in bulk, at least 1 hour.

In the meantime, prepare the filling. Sauté the diced onions in the oil until light golden brown. While the flame is still on, add in the breadcrumbs and continue to sauté another few minutes, so that the crumbs also become coated with oil and start to get a little bit crispy.

Turn off the flame. Add in the salt and pepper and toss to coat evenly. Set aside to cool down until use.

Punch the dough down and knead for five minutes. Divide the dough into four equal parts. Roll out each section in a large circle and slice it with a knife into four or eight sections, pizza-style. Four sections will make much larger croissants, eight will make smaller ones.

Place a heaping tablespoon (or half the amount for the smaller croissants) of the onion mixture into the center of each slice.

Starting from the wider end, roll up the slice of dough inwards.

After it is rolled, gently shape it into a "U" shape and lay it down on the baking sheet.

Allow the croissants to rise for 45 minutes. They should rise to at least double their size. About 20 minutes prior to baking time, preheat the oven to 350˚F / 180˚C. Brush them with egg glaze. Bake for 25 minutes or until the croissants are golden brown.

Filled Doughnuts (a.k.a. "Sufganiot")

These are a traditional Chanukah treat

- 7 cups white flour
- ¼ tsp. salt
- ¾ cup sugar
- 3 eggs
- ½ cup oil
- 50 gm. fresh yeast granules
- 1 packet (1 T.) vanilla sugar
- 3–4 T. orange juice
- 1 cup warm water

Place the flour, salt, and sugar in a mixing bowl. Add the eggs and oil and knead for two minutes until crumbly. Make a well in the center of this mixture and sprinkle in the yeast granules, vanilla sugar, juice, and warm water. Cover the bowl and let it sit for 10 minutes. The yeast should have begun activating.

Knead until a soft and pliable dough is formed. If the dough is too hard, add a few drops more of water and oil until it is a uniformly smooth dough. If the dough is too wet, just add a bit more flour to it. Smear your hands with a fine layer of oil and pat the dough all over with your hands.

Cover the bowl and allow the dough to rise for 30 minutes.

This looks like a very small amount of dough but in reality it makes quite a lot of doughnuts. (at least 40) Since doughnuts cannot be frozen and are only good eaten right away, unless you are expecting a tremendous crowd, it does not pay to double this recipe.

Punch the dough down and you are ready to begin.

Roll out a section of the dough so that it is thin, but not transparent.

Then press a round glass gently into half of the dough, but do not press down hard enough to cut them out yet.

In the center of each round, add the fillings of your choice.

Some great ideas are chocolate chips, jelly, caramel, chocolate cream, or even peanut butter! Gently fold the other half of the dough over the little bumps and circles.

Blessing: "mezonos"

Take the glass used in the first step, press it down firmly around each bump (i.e. your filling) and twist while cutting it out.

This will seal the filling into the center of each doughnut. Keep doing this until they are all filled and twisted shut. Leave them to rise on the counter or on a piece of parchment baking paper for 30 minutes, until they look puffed up.

Now comes the frying part. Fill a dairy pot with oil until halfway full.

Great Tip: Before beginning to fry the doughnuts, put

a piece of carrot into the oil. It will keep the oil from turning black and burning or ruining the doughnuts as they are frying.

Fry doughnuts in the hot oil for 3–5 minutes until golden brown. Flip them over and continue to fry on

the second side. When the second side is also golden, use a slotted spoon to

remove each doughnut onto a plate lined with paper towels. The paper towels absorb the excess oil.

After each doughnut cools down for about 5-7 minutes, sprinkle it with powdered sugar and bite in!

The Missing Dough

I WAS STANDING BY MY KITCHEN COUNTER, having made a large challah dough, and was getting ready to do the mitzvah of separating challah. As I was moving around the kitchen, my young daughter pulled up a chair and climbed up on it, perching herself right near the counter so she could have a really good view of what I was doing. Her eyes lit up as she saw my large bowl of dough. How she loved to squish and shape challah dough alongside me! And even more so, how she dearly loved to sneak bits of challah dough into her cute little mouth! I thought it was hilarious to watch her, she all the time thinking to herself that she was actually fooling me and managing to quickly eat some dough while "Mommy isn't looking."

So there she was, happily standing on a chair near me by the counter. She watched intently as I made my brachah and then separated off the required piece...and then placed it on a piece of aluminum foil so I could burn it.

I turned my head for a few minutes, intent on the personal prayers I was saying following the act of the mitzvah, completely engrossed in what I was doing. Then I got busy with the last few steps of organizing myself before starting the shaping process.

I searched around for that piece of dough on the foil; I wanted to burn it right away. I thought I had placed it on the counter near the bowl of dough...but it was nowhere to be found. I still don't know what took me so long to figure this out, but then I realized, to my horror, that my adorable little daughter was surreptitiously chewing on something...gooey and white! With a wicked little look in her eyes! Oh no – she ate the actual piece of sanctified challah! I didn't know whether to laugh or cry, or both. That piece is considered unkosher – treif is more the word – and it was supposed to be disposed of, not eaten!! And did that mean that my mitzvah was invalid? Did I have to separate dough all over again??? What a question! Who to ask? If I call a Rabbi, he'll either laugh me out of town or berate me for being such a fool of a mother!

I didn't know what to do so I finally plucked up my courage to call a Rabbi and just ask already. I was so worked up over the whole thing that I almost cried on the phone. When the Rabbi finally clearly understood from me what had happened, I could hear him trying to hold back his own laughter. He didn't want to make me feel stupid, but, hey, this **was** pretty funny. It certainly isn't your average, everyday "ask the Rabbi" kind of question!

"Well, I don't really think you can get your piece of challah back anymore, can you?" he managed to say with a straight voice. "It's already destroyed at this point. However, you needn't worry about your dough; it's fine, and you don't have to do the mitzvah again. And your daughter – she's still plenty kosher as well. Maybe next time, put your challah just a little bit more out of reach..."

(For verification of this law, see the Appendix at the end of this book, "Halachos of Separating Challah," page 198, section 8, paragraph number 11.)

After that I calmed down, and even managed to find the humor in it. A short while later when I told it over to a friend of mine, we both laughed uproariously at the ridiculousness of the whole situation.

And my little girl? You'd think she had enough dough for one day after that nice-sized piece she managed to sneak down. Not so. I caught her a few minutes later with her hand poised near the dough yet again...

Traditional Bobka

Blessing: "mezonos"

An incredible old-fashioned yeast dough that will come out delicious every time. Loaded with taste, calories, and everything that's far too scrumptious!

Hungarians also call this "kokosh cake."

This recipe makes 4 large bobka loaves, or 7 small ones.

DOUGH:

- *1 cup warm water*
- *1 cup orange juice at room temperature*
- *50 gm. fresh yeast*
- *1 ½ cups margarine*
- *1 cup sugar*
- *8 cups flour*
- *2 eggs*
- *2 egg yolks*
- *1 T. vanilla sugar*

In a small bowl, combine the orange juice with the warm water. Add the yeast and let it bubble up and start to activate. Set aside. Place the margarine and sugar in the bowl of your mixer and mix together until it resembles crumbs. Make a well in the center and add everything else. Knead together until it becomes a slightly sticky dough.

Separate challah without a *brachah*. Cover the bowl and let it rise until double in bulk, about an hour. Punch down and you are "ready to roll."

FILLING:

- *¾ cup cocoa*
- *1 ½ cups sugar*
- *¾ cup powdered sugar*
- *2 T. vanilla sugar*

Combine these together by hand in a bowl.

CRUMBS:

- *1 cup flour*
- *½ cup margarine*
- *¾ cup sugar*

Combine these in a bowl, and crumble together by hand until it resembles fine crumbs. Reserve for later use.

Divide the dough into four portions for four large bobkas, or seven portions for seven smaller-sized ones. Bobkas have more shape and height if they are baked in loaf pans, so if you have them, then either line them with parchment baking paper or spray them with cooking spray to prepare them for your rolled loaves.

Lightly grease your working surface with some oil. Pour more oil into a small bowl and leave it nearby; you will need this to smear on the rolled-out dough before sprinkling on the filling ingredients. Divide each piece of dough into two. Using a rolling pin, roll out the dough to a medium-sized oval, making sure it is not too thick or too thin. *It will break and leak when filled if you roll it too thinly.* With a pastry brush, brush the dough with a fine layer of oil, from the center outwards.

Do not brush oil at the very edges of the dough. Sprinkle the cocoa filling generously all over the oiled dough, up to just before the edges, the same as the oil.

Close up the edges of the dough on the shorter sides so that the filling will not spill out; then roll up the

dough from the long side, jelly-roll style, and bring the last bit of dough up to meet the roll.

Make two such rolls, then twist them together and place them in the loaf pans you prepared earlier. Leave to rise, slightly covered, for 45 minutes, until about double in size.

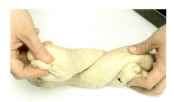

Preheat the oven to 350°F / 180°C. After the loaves have risen, sprinkle the crumb mixture all over

the top of each loaf just before sliding them into the oven.

The topping will fall all over, but that is okay; a lot of it will also stick to the loaf as it bakes. Bake for 40–45 minutes for smaller loaves, a bit longer for larger loaves, until golden brown on top. Leave to cool in the pan for 10 minutes, then remove the bobkas to a wire rack to cool completely.

Freeze until use or else you will not have anything to put away at all! These are quite dangerous straight out of the oven, so you may want to make them on a day when you are alone in the house.

Margarine-Reduced Bobka

Blessing: "mezonos"

This recipe makes a large amount, between 7–10 large bobkas, depending on the size you choose to make them.

Place flour, margarine, and eggs into the mixer. Mix together a bit. Add the yeast and everything else. Knead together until a smooth dough is formed. Separate challah with a *brachah*. Let the dough rise for 1 hour or place the dough in a large garbage bag, remove the air, and put it in the refrigerator for several hours or overnight.

Punch down and begin to shape.

Separate the dough into sections and roll out and fill the same way as shown in the previous bobka recipe.

Below are two filling ideas. This dough does not need to be smeared with oil prior to filling it; the oil is incorporated into the filling instead. Each filling makes enough for the entire recipe; if you want to try out both flavors, simply divide the filling measurements in half.

CHOCOLATE FILLING:

- 2 cups cocoa
- 6 cups sugar
- 10 T. vanilla sugar
- 1 T. lemon juice
- 1 tsp. cinnamon

Mix everything together in a bowl. Add in approximately ½ cup of oil and stir by hand until it resembles a loose paste.

Smear this onto the rolled-out dough pieces and roll up as in the previous recipe.

CINNAMON FILLING:

- 3 cups powdered sugar
- 3 cups regular sugar
- 4–6 T. ground cinnamon

Mix together in a bowl and add approximately ½ cup of oil until it resembles a thick paste.

Smear and roll up as directed above. You may add more cinnamon and sugar to the top of the bobka as well, once it is risen.

Allow bobkas to rise as in previous recipe. After they have risen, they may be sprinkled with crumbs, as described in the previous recipe, just before baking.

If you are able to obtain very fine whole wheat pastry flour, this dough would work wonderfully as a whole wheat bobka recipe.

Place the dry ingredients in a bowl and mix. Add in the oil a bit at a time and toss with a fork until it resembles a crumb mixture. *The whole one cup of oil may or may not be necessary.* Sprinkle onto the risen bobkas.

Bake at 350°F / 180°C for 45 minutes to 1 hour, until golden and firm.

Let cool in pans for 10 minutes, then remove to wire racks to cool completely. Freeze until use.

This amount will require separating challah with a bracha. You may halve the recipe if this is too many bobkas for your family.

Sweet Zucchini Bread

The blessing recited when eating this sweet zucchini bread is "mezonos"

This "bread" has no yeast and is more the consistency of cake. This recipe will fill two standard loaf pans or three small ones.

Beat eggs, vanilla, oil, and sugar together until thick. Add in the pineapple, zucchini, baking soda, baking powder, salt, and cinnamon. Then add in the flour, and on top of that, the raisins and walnuts.

It's always best to add the raisins on top of the flour, as once the raisins are coated with flour, they will not sink down to the bottom of whatever cake or muffin they are in, where they may burn.

Mix until this is completely blended together and resembles a thick batter.

Pour into loaf pans that have been lined with parchment baking paper and bake at 350°F/180°C for 45 minutes to 1 hour.

They are done when a cake tester or knife inserted into the middle comes out clean and only very slightly sticky.

These loaves stay moist and slightly sticky inside. Slice and serve, or freeze for later use.

Tasty Homemade Breadcrumbs

Another great way to use up old challah is to create your own breadcrumbs from them.

The next day, put them through the food processor and blend until they become fine crumbs.

Store in an airtight container or zippered storage bag in the freezer until use.

These breadcrumbs make an excellent coating for breaded chicken or cutlets; simply add spices to them and coat the chicken pieces.

Spread out the pieces of bread on a baking tray and toast them in a hot oven at 350°F / 180°C for 15-20 minutes.

Then turn off the heat and allow them to sit in the oven overnight to dry out.

Croutons

Making your own real-bread croutons is fun and easy and makes a great extra treat that can be thrown over individual salad plates directly before eating.

Take slices of day-old challah or bread and cut them into small cubes.

After all the bread has been cubed, place it in a large bowl and douse generously with olive oil.

Sprinkle well with granulated garlic, onion powder, and parsley flakes.

Toss to coat and place croutons on a lined baking tray.

Slide into a preheated 350°F/180°C oven and toast them until they are golden brown.

Since these croutons are made straight from toasted bread, please be aware that their blessing would be "ha-motzi."

Calzones (a.k.a. Pizza Roll-Ups)

When eating these calzones, the blessing recited over them is the same as for pizza. See page 15.

This is a fun and easy idea that anyone can do, the same day they make a challah dough, for a simple and enjoyable meal for the whole family ...

Take a piece of dough about the size of the palm of your hand and roll it out.

Smear each piece of dough with tomato sauce and sprinkle some oregano on top.

Take an assortment of pizza fillings such as grated cheese, sliced olives, onions, mushrooms— even crumbled tofu—and spread it all over the sauce.

Fold over the edges on the sides and then roll up the dough the long way, carefully keeping everything inside.

Allow the calzones to rise on a greased baking sheet or pan for 30-40 minutes. Brush with egg glaze if desired or only oil.

Bake at 350°F/180°C, bake until golden brown and firm on top and bottom, approximately 20 minutes.

Bite in and enjoy!

Pizza

For information about which blessing to say on pizza, see page 15.

DOUGH:

For 2 larger-sized pizzas or 4 personal pizza pies

- *3½ cups flour*
- *1 tsp. salt*
- *1 tsp. sugar*
- *1 oz. or 25–30 gm. fresh yeast*
- *1 ⅓ cups warm water*

Mix all ingredients together until it forms a smooth dough. Grease a bowl and turn the dough into it. Cover it with plastic and then a damp towel to rise for 30 minutes. Punch down and divide into two portions for two large pizzas, or four portions for four small ones. Roll each piece out in a large circle and place into the pan of choice.

SAUCE:

- *2½ cups tomato sauce (if using paste, add some water to it to make it less thick)*
- *1 T. oil*
- *½ tsp. pepper*
- *2 tsp. salt*
- *1 tsp. oregano*

Mix together and spread over the rolled-out pizza pies.

Now you can have lots of fun with all sorts of toppings:

- *shredded cheese*
- *sliced green olives*
- *sliced black olives*
- *sliced red and green peppers*
- *sliced mushrooms*
- *chopped onions*

Sprinkle grated cheese all over the sauce.

Add toppings of your choice on top of the grated cheese, according to your taste.

Bake at 350°F / 180°C for approximately 20-25 minutes until the pizza is crispy on the bottom and bubbly on top. Enjoy!

Halachos
of Separating
Challah

The following is a brief summary of the basic laws of separating challah. Due to limitations of space, many details could not be included in this work. Extensive and detailed coverage of this important topic can be found in **Guidelines to Candle Lighting & Separating Challah** *(Targum Press, www.targum.com), where the source material for these laws can also be found. This book may be purchased online or wherever Jewish books are sold worldwide.*

Among the Torah personalities who have given their blessings and approbations to the Guidelines series are: Rabbi Chaim Pinchas Scheinberg, Rosh HaYeshivah Torah Ore; Rabbi Pesach Eliyahu Falk, author of "Modesty — An Adornment for Life"; and Rabbi Zev Leff, Rav of Moshav Matisyahu.

© Rabbi Elozor Barclay and Rabbi Yitzchok Jaeger

1. Introduction

1. When a person prepares a large quantity of dough for baking (see Section 4, p.190), he is obligated to perform the mitzvah of SEPARATING a small piece of dough and sanctifying it. This piece is called challah.

2. Challah must be separated from any type of BAKED FOOD made from certain types of flour, if a sufficiently large quantity is prepared. This includes cakes, cookies, biscuits, matzah, etc. **Note:** This summary of laws is for bread only. For cakes, etc., see *Guidelines to Challah.*

3. According to the Sages, this is one of the few mitzvos for which the entire world was created. If challah is not separated when required, the grains are cursed and there is a shortage of food. But if the mitzvah is performed, the grains will grow in abundance and one's house will be blessed.

4. The Sages gave the privilege of performing this mitzvah to the WOMAN. Together with the other two mitzvos — family purity and kindling the Shabbos lights — the separation of challah completes the trio of mitzvos given specifically to women. When a woman is experiencing the perilous throes of childbirth, the merit of these three mitzvos stands by her for a safe and successful delivery.

5. Originally, the challah was given as a gift to a Kohen, who would eat it when in a state of ritual purity. Today, when everyone is assumed to be ritually impure, the challah is DESTROYED. (See Section 8, p.198)

6. The mitzvah of separating challah may be performed equally on any weekday, and women are encouraged to do so whenever it is convenient.

7. It is praiseworthy to bake challahs on *erev Shabbos* in order to perform the mitzvah of separating challah, thereby rectifying the sin of Adam and Chava, which occurred on *erev Shabbos*. In addition, it is a greater honor of Shabbos to use homemade challahs rather than those bought from a bakery.

8. Some women perform the mitzvah when nearing the time of childbirth, so that they will merit a safe birth. There is also a special mitzvah on *erev Yom Tov*.

2. Types of Dough

1. Challah must be taken from dough made only from flour of the five PRINCIPAL GRAINS. These are: wheat, barley, spelt, oats, and rye.

2. The mitzvah of challah applies to any combination of the five principal types of flour. (Oat flakes combine, even though they have not been ground into flour.)

3. If one mixes wheat flour with rice flour, challah must be separated unless there is sixty times more rice than wheat. A *brachah* should not be recited unless the wheat flour alone is the decisive quantity.

4. Challah may only be separated with a *brachah* if, besides the decisive quantity of flour, the dough contains at least one of the following primary liquids: water, wine or grape juice, olive oil, honey, or milk.
   If none of these liquids are used, challah is separated without a *brachah*. In order to be able to recite the *brachah*, it is correct to add one of these liquids to the ingredients. It should be noted that many fruit juices contain water, even if they claim to be 100 percent pure.

5. If water is used, even one drop is sufficient. If one of the other liquids is used, this must constitute the majority of all the liquid ingredients.

6. In order to recite a *brachah*, the dough must be baked.
   If the dough is to be boiled or fried (e.g. doughnuts), a *brachah* is not recited. If one intends to boil or fry the dough, he should bake a small amount, in order to be able to recite the *brachah*.

7. If the dough is to be first boiled and then baked (e.g. bagels), challah is separated with a *brachah*.

3. Baking

1. The dough need not be BAKED on the day that it is made, but may be stored in a refrigerator or freezer until one wishes to bake it. However, the *brachah* may not be recited unless the appropriate quantity of dough is baked at ONE SESSION.

   For example, if one's custom is to recite a *brachah* for 1.67 kilo of flour and a dough was made from 3 kilo, one may not recite the *brachah* unless 1.67 kilo is baked at one session.

   The remaining part of the dough may be stored for another occasion. However, if the dough was divided into two halves of 1.5 kilo, and each half was baked on a different day, the *brachah* may not be recited.

2. It is not necessary to bake all the dough at once. As long as the dough is baked in one session, one may bake small portions in the oven in succession.

3. If the decisive quantity is made, challah should be separated with a *brachah*, even if some or all of the bread is given away.

4. If some of the dough is given to other people, there is no mitzvah of challah, unless one keeps for oneself an amount that requires separating challah. For instance, a teacher wishes to demonstrate to a class of girls how to make challah (for Shabbos). If she kneads a large amount of dough and gives to each girl a portion to braid and take home to bake, there is no mitzvah to separate challah unless she retains the required amount for herself.

5. If one intends to divide a large amount of dough into two parts and flavor one part differently, challah must be separated. However, a *brachah* should not be recited unless one part is itself large enough to require a *brachah*.

4. Quantities

1. There are many opinions about the QUANTITY OF FLOUR required to separate challah. The custom is to use a smaller measure for the separation of challah without a *brachah*, and a larger measure for the separation with a *brachah*.

2. If a dough contains less than 2 lbs., 10 oz. (1.2 kilo) of flour, challah should not be separated.

   For 2 lbs., 10 oz. to 3 lbs., 10 oz. (1.2–1.67 kilo) of flour, challah should be separated without a *brachah*.

   For 3 lbs., 10 oz. to 5 lbs. (1.67–2.25 kilo) of flour, challah should be separated. Some people recite a *brachah*, and some do not.

   For more than 5 lbs. (2.25 kilo) of flour, challah should be separated with a *brachah*.

3. The equivalent weights in kilos are:

   2 lbs., 10 oz. = 1.2 kilo

   3 lbs., 10 oz. = 1.67 kilo

   5 lbs. = 2.25 kilo

4. The flour should be measured by weight, and NOT by using a cup measure. Nevertheless, as a rough guide, the following are APPROXIMATE equivalents:

   8 American cups = 1.2 kilo

   14 American cups = 1.67 kilo

   19 American cups = 2.25 kilo

5. The flour may be weighed before or after sifting.

6. There are two basic types of whole wheat flour. In one type, the bran is not removed during the sifting, and is included in the required amount of flour. Since bran is lighter than flour, this causes a reduction of the overall weight required for separation by approximately 3.5 percent. The approximate amounts for this type of flour are:

   For 2 lbs., 8 oz. to 3 lbs., 8 oz. (1.16–1.6 kilo) of flour, challah should be separated without a *brachah*.

   For 3 lbs., 8 oz. to 4 lbs., 13 oz. (1.6–2.2 kilo) of flour, challah should be separated. Some people recite a *brachah*, and some do not.

   For more than 2.2 kilo of flour, challah should be separated with a *brachah*.

7. In the second type of whole wheat flour, some of the bran is removed and subsequently mixed into the flour again. The returned bran is not included in the required amount, and a much larger weight of flour is therefore required. No figures can be given for the second type, due to the large variations that exist.

8. Accurate measurements of rye, spelt, barley, and oat flours have revealed that they are all lighter than wheat flour by approximately 15 to 20 percent. It is therefore suggested to separate challah from the following amounts:

For 2 lbs., 3 oz. to 3 lbs., 2 oz. (1–1.4 kilo) of flour, challah should be separated without a *brachah*.

For 3 lbs., 2 oz. to 4 lbs., 3 oz. (1.4–1.9 kilo) of flour, challah should be separated. Some people recite a *brachah*, and some do not.

For more than 4 lbs., 3 oz. (1.9 kilo) of flour, challah should be separated with a *brachah*.

9. Flour that is added to the dough to improve its texture or to aid in easy rolling should be included in the calculation of the amount of flour used. However, in most cases the amount is negligible and only if the total amount of flour borders on a decisive quantity should one postpone the mitzvah of separating challah until one is certain that no more flour will be used.

10. If challah was separated with a *brachah*, and then more flour added, nothing needs to be done. If challah was separated without a *brachah* and the amount of flour was bordering on a decisive quantity and then more flour added, one should separate challah again without a *brachah*.

11. It is a greater mitzvah to separate challah with a *brachah* than without. Therefore, it is better to make challah dough in larger quantities, in order to be able to perform the mitzvah of separating challah, even if one will do so less frequently.

12. However, it is better to bake a smaller quantity each week if the family prefers freshly baked challahs rather than ones that have been frozen and defrosted. Even if this entails forfeiting the *brachah*, or the entire mitzvah of separating challah, nevertheless the mitzvah of honoring Shabbos with freshly baked challahs takes priority.

13. If one makes dough in a mixer whose bowl does not hold 2 lbs., 10 oz. (1.2 kilo) of flour, she may make more than one batch of dough and mix them together. The dough must be combined in one of two ways to perform the mitzvah. The first way is if the doughs are brought together, and stuck to each other, to the extent that one tears dough from the other when separated.

Alternatively, the doughs are put into one container. The container should have sufficient depth that each piece of dough is at least partially inside. None of the pieces of dough should be completely above the rim of the container.

The doughs can also be combined by putting them all inside a large plastic or paper bag. Similarly, a large cardboard box may be used. Ideally, the doughs should touch each other inside the container.

14. Similarly, two or more doughs, or breads that were made at different times, can be combined unintentionally to make the correct quantity to separate challah. The many details and ramifications of this rule are beyond the scope of this work and can be found in *Guidelines to Candle Lighting and Separating Challah*.

5. Who Separates Challah

1. Although the main obligation is on the owner of the dough, i.e. the husband, the Sages gave the privilege of performing this mitzvah to the woman.

2. The husband may separate challah, but he must first ask permission from his wife.

3. The wife may honor another woman with the mitzvah, and she does not need to ask permission from her husband to do so.

4. A child below bar/bas mitzvah age may not separate challah.

5. If a child separated challah, it is valid if the separation was done by a boy aged twelve or a girl aged eleven, if the child understands what he/she is doing. Otherwise, the separation must be repeated by an adult.

6. If a child made the dough, challah must be separated as usual by an adult.

*Artwork by
Esther Schwalbe
schwalbe @013.net*

6. When to Separate Challah

1. In Eretz Yisrael, it is forbidden to eat from the dough before separating challah. In the diaspora it is usually permitted to eat from it, even after it has been baked, provided one leaves a portion from which challah is separated. Nevertheless, it is correct to separate challah first.

2. In Eretz Yisrael, one may not taste the dough before it has been separated in order to see if it needs more flavoring. After the flour and liquid have been fully mixed, one is obligated to separate challah and then they may taste the dough.

3. In the diaspora, if two or more small quantities of dough or bread are combined to create an obligation to take challah, one may not eat from the combined foods until challah has been separated.

4. Challah should be separated as soon as one has completely finished making the dough. One should not wait until the dough has risen. Similarly, one should not put the dough into the refrigerator or freezer without separating challah.

5. If a woman makes the quantity of dough that obligates her to take challah without a *brachah*, she should perform the mitzvah immediately. It is incorrect to postpone the mitzvah, even if her intention is to make another dough at a later date to combine with the first, in order to gain the *brachah*. However, if the second dough will be made on the same day as the first, the mitzvah may be delayed until both doughs are combined.

6. A mother may delay separating challah in order to teach her daughter how to perform the mitzvah, provided that she will separate challah from the dough before it is baked.
   She may not first bake the dough without separating challah, intending to show her daughter how to separate challah from the baked bread.

7. If a woman baked the dough before separating challah, she must separate challah from the bread as soon as she remembers.

8. If some of the bread was already eaten, this is an error in Eretz Yisrael, but in the diaspora no wrong has been done. In any event, challah must be separated from the remaining bread as soon as possible.

9. If some or all of the bread was given to other people, this is an error even in the diaspora, and a *rav* should be consulted.

10. If a woman cannot remember whether she separated challah, she may assume that she did so if she performs the mitzvah on a regular basis.
    Nevertheless, it is recommended that she separates a tiny piece again without a *brachah*.

7. How to Separate Challah

1. Some have the custom to give *tzedakah* before separating challah.

2. The custom is to stand when separating challah if one is able to, especially if one is reciting the *brachah*.

3. When a *brachah* is required, one should do the following:

   (a) SEPARATE a small piece of the dough;

   (b) RECITE the *brachah*;

   (c) DECLARE the separated piece to be challah;

   (d) DISPOSE of the challah.

   When a *brachah* is not required, the second step is omitted. Some have the custom to recite the *brachah* before separating a piece.

4. The custom is to SEPARATE a piece the SIZE of a *kezayis*, i.e. half a standard egg. Since this piece must be destroyed, it is unnecessary and wasteful to separate a larger piece than this.

5. If one separated less than a *kezayis*, the mitzvah has been properly fulfilled and should not be repeated.

6. If one buys bread or receives it as a gift and wishes to separate challah in case this was not done, it is sufficient to separate a tiny amount. In this situation, there is no custom to separate a *kezayis*.

7. The main custom is to SAY the following *brachah*:

בָּרוּךְ אַתָּה יְיָ
אֱלֹהֵינוּ מֶלֶךְ הָעוֹלָם
אֲשֶׁר קִדְּשָׁנוּ בְּמִצְוֹתָיו
וְצִוָּנוּ לְהַפְרִישׁ חַלָּה

Baruch Ata Adonoy Eloheinu Melech ha-olam, asher keedshanu be-mitzvosav vetzeevanu lehafreesh challah.

Blessed are You, our G-d, King of the Universe, Who has sanctified us with His commandments and commanded us to separate challah.

Some have the custom to add the words תְּרוּמָה or מִן הָעִסָּה

The same *brachah* is recited whether one separates challah from dough or bread.

8. It is preferable not to recite the *brachah* of shehecheyanu when performing the mitzvah for the first time. Nevertheless, it would be praiseworthy to find an opportunity to recite the *brachah* by wearing a new garment or eating a new fruit.

9. One should DECLARE the separated piece to be challah by saying

הֲרֵי זוֹ חַלָּה

or "this is challah."

10. If one did not say the declaration, the mitzvah has still been fulfilled only if a *brachah* is recited. Nevertheless, it is more correct to say the declaration, especially if one separates the piece before reciting the *brachah*.

   If a *brachah* was not recited, but the piece was declared to be challah in one's mind, the mitzvah has been fulfilled, although not in the ideal way. If the *brachah* was not recited, and the piece was not declared to be challah in one's mind, the mitzvah has not been fulfilled and the declaration must be said.

11. If one forgot to recite the *brachah*, it is too late to recite it if the piece has already been declared to be challah.

12. It is forbidden to speak after reciting the *brachah* until after the declaration.

13. After the declaration, the custom is to say the prayer that is said at the conclusion of *Shemoneh Esrei*:

יְהִי רָצוֹן מִלְּפָנֶיךָ יְיָ אֱלֹהֵינוּ וֵאלֹהֵי אֲבוֹתֵינוּ, שֶׁיִּבָּנֶה בֵּית הַמִּקְדָּשׁ בִּמְהֵרָה בְיָמֵינוּ, וְתֵן חֶלְקֵנוּ בְּתוֹרָתֶךָ, וְשָׁם נַעֲבָדְךָ בְּיִרְאָה כִּימֵי עוֹלָם וּכְשָׁנִים קַדְמוֹנִיּוֹת. וְעָרְבָה לַיְיָ מִנְחַת יְהוּדָה וִירוּשָׁלָיִם, כִּימֵי עוֹלָם וּכְשָׁנִים קַדְמוֹנִיּוֹת.

MAY IT BE YOUR WILL, Eternal, our G-d, and the G-d of our forefathers, that the Temple be rebuilt speedily, in our days. Let our portion be together in Your Torah. And there we will serve You, with reverence and awe, as in days gone by, as in years long ago.
And there we will sacrifice to Hashem, our G-d, the offerings of Yehudah and Yerushalayim, as in days gone by, as in years long ago.

14. It is appropriate to pray for righteous and G-d-fearing children (see next page).

15. When reciting the *brachah* and declaration, the separated piece should be placed next to the remaining dough or bread.

16. If one wishes to hold the piece, the hand should preferably be held near the remaining dough or bread.

Prayer after Separating Challah:

וִיהִי רָצוֹן מִלְּפָנֶיךָ שֶׁהַמִּצְוָה שֶׁל הַפְרָשַׁת חַלָּה תִּתְחַשֵּׁב כְּאִלּוּ
קִיַּמְתִּיהָ בְּכָל פְּרָטֶיהָ וְדִקְדּוּקֶיהָ, וְתֵחָשֵׁב הֲרָמַת הַחַלָּה שֶׁאֲנִי
מְרִימָה כְּמוֹ הַקָּרְבָּן שֶׁהֻקְרַב עַל הַמִּזְבֵּחַ שֶׁנִּתְקַבֵּל בְּרָצוֹן, וּכְמוֹ
שֶׁלְּפָנִים הָיְתָה הַחַלָּה נְתוּנָה לַכֹּהֵן וְהָיְתָה זוֹ לְכַפָּרַת עֲוֹנוֹת, כָּךְ
תִּהְיֶה לְכַפָּרָה לַעֲוֹנוֹתַי, וְאָז אֶהְיֶה כְּאִלּוּ נוֹלַדְתִּי מֵחָדָשׁ נְקִיָּה
מֵחֵטְא וְעָוֹן – וְאוּכַל לְקַיֵּם מִצְוַת שַׁבַּת קֹדֶשׁ וְהַיָּמִים הַטּוֹבִים,
עִם בַּעְלִי (וִילָדֵינוּ) לִהְיוֹת נִזּוֹנִים מִקְּדֻשַּׁת הַיָּמִים הָאֵלֶּה,
וּמֵהַשְׁפָּעָתָהּ שֶׁל מִצְוַת חַלָּה יִהְיוּ יְלָדֵינוּ נִזּוֹנִים תָּמִיד מִיָּדָיו שֶׁל
הַקָּדוֹשׁ בָּרוּךְ הוּא בְּרֹב רַחֲמָיו וַחֲסָדָיו, וּבְרֹב אַהֲבָה, וְשֶׁתִּתְקַבֵּל
מִצְוַת חַלָּה כְּאִלּוּ נָתַתִּי מַעֲשֵׂר, וּכְשֵׁם שֶׁהִנְנִי מְקַיֶּמֶת מִצְוַת
חַלָּה בְּכָל לֵב, כָּךְ יִתְעוֹרְרוּ רַחֲמָיו שֶׁל הַקָּדוֹשׁ בָּרוּךְ הוּא
לְשָׁמְרֵנִי מִצַּעַר וּמִמַּכְאוֹבִים כָּל הַיָּמִים, אָמֵן:

Illustration by Esther Schwalbe, Swan Calligraphics • Schwalbe@barak-online.net

Prayer after Separating Challah:

MAY IT BE YOUR WILL, *Eternal, our G-d, that the commandment of separating challah be considered as if I had performed it with all its details and ramifications. May my elevation of the challah be comparable to the sacrifice that was offered on the altar, which was acceptable and pleasing. Just as giving the challah to the Kohein in former times served to atone for sins, so may it atone for mine, and make me like a person reborn without sins. May it enable me to observe the holy Sabbath (or festival of ...) with my husband (and our children) and to become imbued with its holiness. May the spiritual influence of the mitzvah of challah enable our children to be constantly sustained by the hands of the Holy One, blessed is He, with His abundant mercy, loving-kindness, and love. Consider the mitzvah of challah as if I have given a tithe. And just as I am fulfilling this mitzvah with all my heart, so may Your compassion be aroused to keep me from sorrow and pain, always. Amen.*

8. Disposing of the Challah

1. The custom is to burn the separated challah. However, if one feels that this is difficult, he may wrap it in one plastic bag and throw it into the garbage.

2. Burning the challah must be done with care. The piece of challah is sanctified, and is forbidden to be eaten like *treif* food. Therefore, anything that it touches while it is hot becomes *treif* and requires kashering, just as one must kasher a utensil that touches hot *treif* food.

3. The challah may be burned on the flames of a gas stove. It should be placed on a piece of foil or in a tin can.

4. The challah must be burned until it has totally turned to ashes. For this reason, it is recommended not to separate a piece larger than necessary.

5. Ideally, the challah should not be placed directly on the ceramic burner or the grate since these would become *treif* from the hot challah.

6. One may hold the challah over the flames with a fork. However, the fork becomes *treif* and requires kashering by fire before resuming its regular use.

If one wishes to use this method of burning, it is recommended to set aside one specific fork which will remain *treif*, and may be used every time without kashering.

7. The challah may be burned on an electric stove if the element becomes red hot, since the element kashers itself at this temperature.

8. For many reasons that are beyond the scope of this summary, it is not recommended to burn the challah in an oven, even if it is wrapped in foil.

9. If one burned the challah in the oven, a *rav* should be consulted regarding the status of the bread and the oven.

10. It is incorrect to freeze the challah until *erev Pesach*, in order to burn the challah in a live fire together with the *chametz*.

11. If the challah was accidentally eaten, this is an error. Nevertheless, the mitzvah of separating challah has been fulfilled and need not be repeated. The remaining bread may be eaten.

12. If the challah became mixed with the remaining dough, a *rav* should be consulted.

9. Shabbos and Yom Tov

1. Under normal circumstances, it is forbidden to separate challah on Shabbos.

2. If one forgot to separate challah before Shabbos, in Eretz Yisrael nothing can be done. The bread may not be eaten until challah is separated after Shabbos, and it is *muktzeh* during Shabbos. In the diaspora, the bread may be eaten, provided that one puts aside a portion from which challah will be separated after Shabbos.

3. It is a mitzvah for a man to gently ask his wife on *erev Shabbos* whether she remembered to separate challah.

   The special Shabbos loaves are known as challahs, in order to remind people to separate challah when necessary. The best time to ask her is close to the time of candle lighting.

4. If she forgot to separate challah and kindled Shabbos lights, she should ask her husband or a child over bar/bas mitzvah age to separate challah for her. The other person may only separate challah if it is before sunset, and he/she has not yet accepted Shabbos.

5. If she only remembers shortly after sunset, the following rules apply: In the diaspora, challah may not be separated until after Shabbos (see 8, below). In Eretz Yisrael, challah may be separated if this bread is important for Shabbos. For example, there is no other bread; there is other bread, but there are no other whole loaves for *lechem mishneh*; there are other whole loaves, but this bread is much tastier.

6. One may separate challah in Eretz Yisrael until thirteen minutes after sunset. However, one may not separate challah if the synagogue to which one belongs has already accepted Shabbos by saying *bo'ee veshalom.*

7. If one mistakenly separated challah on Shabbos, this is a transgression. Nevertheless the mitzvah has been fulfilled and the bread may be eaten.

8. In the diaspora, one may not separate challah on Friday after sunset, nor on Shabbos. Instead, one may eat most of the bread on Shabbos before challah has been separated.

   A piece of bread a little more than a *kezayis* must be put aside until *motzaei Shabbos*. On *motzaei Shabbos*, a piece the size of a *kezayis* should be separated from the remaining bread and declared as challah.

   One must not declare the entire piece of remaining bread as challah.

9. The laws of separating challah on Yom Tov are, practically speaking, the same as for Shabbos.

Measurements and Conversions

COMMON ABBREVIATIONS:

Ounce = oz.

Pound = lb.

Teaspoon = tsp./ t.

Tablespoon = T.

Cup = c.

Pint = pt.

Quart = qt.

Gallon = gal.

OVEN TEMPERATURES:

Very cool	250–275°F	130–140°C
Cool	300°F	150°C
Warm	325°F	170°C
Moderate	350°F	180°C
Moderately hot	375–400°F	190–200°C
Hot	425°F	220°C
Very hot	450–475°F	230–250°C

TEMPERATURE:

Celsius x 9÷5 + 32

= Fahrenheit

YEAST CONVERSION MEASUREMENTS:

Compressed Yeast	Instant Active Dry Yeast
3 oz. (90 gm.)	1 oz. (30 gm.)
6 oz. (180 gm.)	2 oz. (60 gm.)
9 oz. (270 gm.)	3 oz. (90 gm.)
12 oz. (360 gm.)	4 oz. (120 gm.)
1 lb. (16 oz.) (480 gm.)	5.28 oz. (158 gm.)
1 lb., 8 oz. (720 gm.)	7.92 oz. (238 gm.)

The companies specializing in yeast packaged for home baking recommend substituting 1 cube compressed yeast (0.6 oz.) for 2¼ tsp. instant active dry yeast.

WEIGHT:

These weight measurements are not exact, but have been rounded off to make your calculations in the kitchen easier.

¼ oz. = 7 gm.

½ oz. = 15 gm.

1 oz. = 30 gm.

2 oz. = 56.70 gm.; *for our purposes, it was rounded to about 50/55 gm.*

4 oz. = ¼ lb = 115 gm.

8 oz. = ½ lb = 225 gm.

12 oz. = ¾ pound = 350 gm.

16 oz. = 1 pound = 450 gm.

2 lbs. = 900 gm.

2¼ lbs. = 1 kg

4½ lbs. = 2 kg

Grams x .035 = Oz.

Kilograms x 2.2 = Lbs.

LINEAR MEASUREMENTS:

0.394 inch = 1 cm.

1 inch = 2.54 cm.

millimeters x .04 = inches

centimeters x .4 = inches

OTHER MEASUREMENTS:

1 T. fresh herbs = 1 tsp. dried herbs

1 tsp. = ⅓ T.

3 teaspoons = 1 T. = ½ fluid ounce

1½ teaspoons = ½ T.

2 T. = ⅛ cup = 1 fluid ounce

4 T. = ¼ cup = 2 fluid oz.

8 T. = ½ cup = 4 fluid oz.

16 T. = 1 cup = 8 fluid oz. = ½ pint

⅓ cup = 5 T. + 1 tsp.

⅜ cup = ¼ cup + 2 T.

½ cup = 8 T. = 4 fluid oz.

⅔ cup = 10 T. + 2 teaspoons

⅝ cup = ½ cup + 2 T.

¾ cup = 12 T. = 6 fluid oz.

⅞ cup = ¾ cup + 2 T.

1 cup = 16 T. = ½ pint = 8 fluid oz.

2 cups = 1 pint = 16 fluid oz.

1 quart = 2 pints = 4 cups = 32 fluid oz.

1 gallon = 4 quarts

VOLUME:

Milliliters x .03 = Fl. Ounces

Liters x 2.1 = Pints

Liters x 1.06 = Quarts

Liters x .26 = Gallons

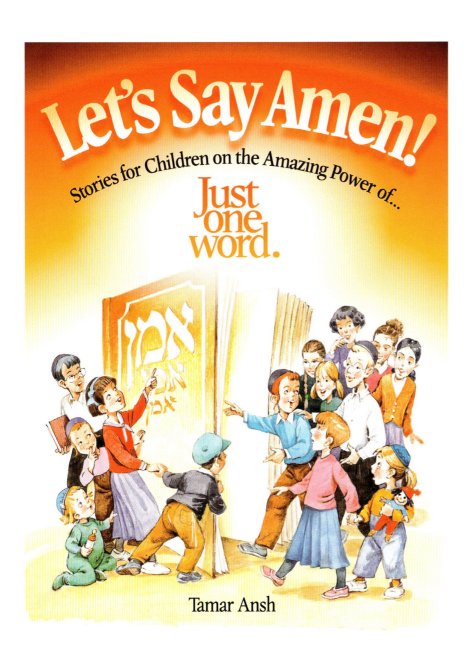

LET'S SAY AMEN !

Stories for Children on the Amazing Power of Just One Word.

By Tamar Ansh

Feldheim Publishers (www.feldheim.com)

If you loved *Just One Word* – the best-selling book that ushered in the "Amen Initiative" all over the Jewish world – why not share the message with your children and grandchildren?!

Adapted for children by Tamar Ansh and enhanced with Tova Katz's gorgeous illustrations, *Let's Say Amen! Stories for Children on the Amazing Power of Just One Word* will spur your children on to new heights in their *avodas Hashem*. They will be inspired by the moving stories made famous in Esther Stern's adult volume – stories about famous rabbis as well as ordinary Jews on the power of saying Amen and *berachos* properly. Tips and *halachos* to help put it all into practice are interspersed throughout the book, making it a complete and comprehensive guide and motivator for integrating this extraordinary idea into your children's lives.

Let your kids be part of the Amen Revolution!

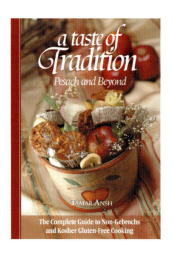

A TASTE OF TRADITION: Pesach and Beyond

The Complete Guide to Non-Gebrochs and Kosher Gluten-Free Cooking

By Tamar Ansh

Feldheim Publishers (www.feldheim.com)

Tamar Ansh brings her expertise in the culinary arts to over 250 mouthwatering recipes that are flavorful, attractive, easy to prepare — and perfect for Pesach and beyond! From soups and salads, side dishes, meats, poultry, and fish to dairy delights, cakes, cookies, and fresh fruit ideas … this tantalizing book invites you to diversify your menu with traditional favorites, holiday classics, and innovative gourmet originals — all non-gebrochs and gluten-free. Complete with full-color photographs and easy-to-follow instructions, *A Taste of Tradition* provides you with dishes to serve and savor — not only on Pesach, but throughout the year.

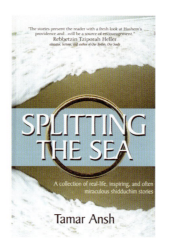

SPLITTING THE SEA

A Collection of Real-life, Inspiring, and Often Miraculous Shidduchim Stories

By Tamar Ansh

Targum Press (www.targum.com)

Singles and *shidduchim*: you may think you've heard it all before … but not until you've read *Splitting the Sea!*

This remarkable collection of true stories and insights is both eye-opening and uplifting. You'll meet people from all walks of life — from around the corner to around the world: real people with real challenges. Sometimes the journey is short and sometimes it is long and difficult, but every life journey is unique — even miraculous.

Jump into the pages of this captivating book and meet people whose insights can truly make a difference to your life. These warm, well-crafted, encouraging stories are guaranteed to strengthen the faith and touch the soul of anyone who reads them.